SUPERFORTRESS
The Boeing B-29

by Steve Birdsall

illustrated by Don Greer
and Rob Stern

squadron/signal publications

ISBN 0-89747-104-0

The cover painting depicts a dawn takeoff assembly by the 498th Bomb Group, 73rd Bomb Wing, based on Isley Field, Saipan, in the Marianas. "Pocahontas", T□23, climbs out in the background while other ships in the group taxi to their takeoff point. From the left, aircraft shown here include: T□21 "Lassie Come Home", T□27 "Torchy", T□22 "Bedroom Eyes" and T□26 "Fay". These early 1945 daylight raids were to prove that the B-29 could be operated over the great distances involved, sometimes well over 3,000 miles round trip.

Acknowledgements

I would like to thank the following individuals - B-29 veterans, staff of The Boeing Company, and members of various organizations for their help and the provision of facts and photos for this book: Rhodes Arnold, George Amthor, Edwin R. Alksne, Colonel Eugene Adams, L. J. Arents, George Birdsong, John T. Bohn, Jeff Brown, Lee Brown, Pete Bowers, Frank B. Bata, Leonard W. Carpi, Edward T. Donnelly, John W. Dennison, A. O. Evans, John Earl, Elden Elliott, Virginia Fincik, Roger A. Freeman, John F. Fuller, Barry Gilkes, Gar S. Gantz, Steve L. Grivno, Harry H. George, Rowland P. Gill, T. C. Griffin, John Gahagan, Robin Gilbert, Edd Halseth, Charles W. Hartke, Charles B. Hawks, Ed Hering, Earl N. Heath, Grant M. Hales, LeRoy Henry, Marv Hooker, Ken Hurley, Marty J. Isham, Ed Jablonski, Francis J. Johnston, Carl A. Janssen, George W. Knight, Paul J. Kelly, Joseph M. Kucera, Al Lloyd, Jim Lynch, Raymond L. Lumbley, John S. LeBlanc, Rick Layman, John Moore, David W. Menard, John H. Mitchell, Charles B. Mayer, Norm Malayney, Tom H. Merrill, Richard M. Morgan, Clyde Matteson, James D. McWethy, John W. McKenna, Eric Olson, Fred J. Olivi, Denny D. Pidhayny, Ray Pritchard, J. Ivan Potts, Edward G. Prunuske, Ed Porada, Larry Reineke, James R. Rook, Larry Redmond, Don Roberts, Ron Reynolds, Leonard W. Smith, Robert H. Stepanek, Frank Smith, Milt Sheppard, Robert E. Sebring, John Swihart, Clay Sandhofer, Vic Seely, Paul D. Stevens, Harold A. Teeter, Ray Tolzmann, Lewis L. Taylor, Al Vacaro, Orley Van Dyke, Gordon S. Williams, Roger Warren, Morris Woodward, Al Williams, Thomas A. Young and Paul H. Zobrist.

-Steve Birdsall

If you have photographs of the aircraft, armor, soldiers or ships of any nation, particularly wartime snapshots, why not share them with us and help make Squadron/Signal's books all the more interesting and complete in the future. Any photograph sent to us will be copied and the original returned. The donor will be fully credited for any photos used. Please send them to: Squadron/Signal Publications Inc., 1115 Crowley Dr., Carrollton, TX 75006.

The once mighty Twentieth Air Force had been reduced to one group, the 19th, when the Korean War broke out. When they moved from Guam to Okinawa in June 1950, the men were told to "pack for a couple of weeks". They would be there for three bitter years. Here, three ships from the 19th head for Korea during the early months of the conflict. (USAF)

The Great Combat Test

The design, production and testing of the B-29 Superfortress was one of the most notable achievements of American Industry. Less than five years after the Boeing Company submitted its design for the world's first truly strategic bomber, the B-29s were laying waste to Japan.

The B-29 was an airplane of superlatives...the world's first pressurized bomber, the world's heaviest production airplane, with the most powerful engines and highest wing loading.

The proof of the design's inherent excellence was the fact that all 3,960 Superfortresses differed little from each other, or from the basic design. In fact, when the first flight of the XB-29 took place on September 21, 1942, sixteen hundred B-29s had already been ordered.

The B-29 program did not run smoothly - there were production delays and bottlenecks, and problems which had to be solved as they arose. All these things cost time, and there was constant pressure, both political and military, to get the B-29s into action.

When the second flight test aircraft crashed in February 1943, killing test pilot Eddie Allen and his crew, the entire multi-million dollar program was in jeopardy. There were those of the opinion that the airplane should be cancelled, but others, in particular the commander of the Army Air Forces, General "Hap" Arnold, believed in the B-29 and fought for it. The Army Air Forces "took over" the project, and by the early months of 1944 Superfortresses were rolling off the production lines at four factories. Boeing's first Wichita production aircraft, 42-6205, was accepted by the Air Force on October 7, 1943 and the company's first Renton-built B-29A, 42-93824, was accepted on New Year's Day of the following year.

The other two companies building B-29s were Martin Aircraft at Omaha, Nebraska and Bell at Marietta in Georgia. Initially they produced five aircraft each under a Boeing Wichita contract, presumably from sub-assemblies shipped from Kansas. The first "all Georgia" Bell aircraft, 42-63352, was accepted on December 30, 1943, while Martin's "first Omaha" B-29, 42-65202, was rolled out in May 1944.

With hand-picked group commanders and a core of seasoned airmen, the first wing, the 58th, was trained, equipped and sent to the China-Burma-India Theater. The combat crews were faced with the task of battle-testing the Superfortress in a theater where conditions could hardly be more difficult. The oven temperatures of India, where the B-29s were based, played havoc with the close-cowled Wright engines, and methods to improve engine cooling and performance assumed top priority. The problem was never entirely solved in the CBI, but constant modifications yielded consistent improvement. Other problems were caused by the fact that the B-29s were intended virtually to supply themselves, transporting their own fuel, bombs and other supplies to forward bases in the Chengtu area of China. This involved grueling flights over the massive Himalaya mountains, the "Hump" route, and B-29s were being worn out simply getting ready to fly combat missions. A partial answer to the problem was the use of B-29 tankers, combat aircraft stripped of armor plate and all armament except the tail turret, and fitted with a total of four bomb bay tanks yielding a gasoline capacity of over 8,000 gallons.

The 58th Wing was able to fly a shakedown mission to Bangkok on June 5, 1944, and ten days later they began their campaign against the Japanese steel industry. The first target was the Imperial Iron and Steel Works at Yawata, on the island of Kyushu; forty-seven B-29s made it to the target and bombed that night, but caused no significant damage. The mission cost seven B-29s, mostly operational losses. The Yawata mission's greatest significance lay in the fact that it was the first time the B-29s had attacked the Japanese homeland.

There was pressure from Washington to increase the frequency and effectiveness of B-29 raids, but as the months passed the results were almost continually disappointing. The wing ranged far and wide, to Anshan, Mukden, Nagasaki, Palembank, Rangoon and Singapore, but was always handicapped by the impossible logistics of their combat theater. The grind over the Hump and the tremendous effort simply to stockpile enough material for missions was heartbreaking, and operational losses continued to be high. The plan to use B-29s from China had always been a compromise, and the main result of these operations was that the Superfortress received a combat shakedown which could hardly have been more arduous.

The B-29s flew their last mission from the forward bases in China in January 1945, and despite the failures the crews could look back on their record with pride. There had been some outstanding successes, particularly against maritime targets at Singapore and an incendiary attack on Hankow, but the B-29s had failed in their primary mission of destroying or crippling Japanese steel production.

High explosive tumbles from the bomb bays of the 468th Group's Mary Ann, **42-24494. The target was Haito, Formosa, on October 16, 1944, and the B-29s carried forty 500lb bombs each. (Ray Tolzmann)**

Major Edwin Loberg's King Size, **from the 462nd Bomb Group, one of the forty-seven B-29s which completed the first Superfortress mission to Japan on June 15, 1944.**

The massive R-3350 engine, the most powerful available and the obvious choice for the B-29. Cooling and other problems plagued the design, particularly in the heat of India, where this 462nd Group aircraft is being maintained. (Hooker)

This 468th Bomb Group aircraft has a replacement tail section from an old camouflaged B-29. (Denny Pidhayny)

Esso Express, 42-6242, a tanker from 468th Bomb Group. During early B-29 operations, fuel was a critical factor, and several B-29s in each group were stripped of all armament but the tail turret, armor plating and other equipment. These cleaner, lighter airplanes were able to offload considerably more fuel than the combat B-29s after flying over the Hump. (Marvin Hooker)

40th Group ground crewmen finish off fitting a brand new engine to Ouija Bird in China. Early expectations of B-29 performance were based on U.S. calculations, which proved unrealistic in the CBI Theater. Conditions were primitive. (USAF)

Genieof the 40th Group in India, with the red tail bands which indentified her as a 25th Squadron aircraft. (Frank Smith)

The 40th Group's Eddie Allen, **42-24579, was "bought" by Boeing Wichita Employees through bond purchases. She was so badly damaged over Tokyo on May 25, 1945 that she could never fly again. Her hulk was used for ditching training. (USAF)**

The 468th Group's Chat'nooga Choo Choo, **in full 58th Wing regalia. Her tail carries the Billy Mitchell flag, and the white tail stripes identify her squadron, the 792nd. Her nose carries markings denoting bombing, photo recon and Hump transport missions. (Pidhayny)**

Meanwhile, the second B-29 wing, the 73rd, had gone to a far more favorable area, the Marianas - a group of islands lying some fifteen hundred miles from the heart of the Japanese homeland. The 73rd flew its first Empire mission on November 24, 1944, to Tokyo; it faced new problems. The high winds and cloud conditions over the Japanese targets hampered high level precision bombing to such a degree that mission after mission failed to achieve the desired results. The ditching rate was high, and the air-sea rescue operation organization was still learning the ropes. Many crews ditched in sight of other B-29s, were seen to leave their airplanes safely, then simply disappeared. For the crews flying the long missions to Japan with marginal fuel reserves, a damaged or malfunctioning engine could mean the difference between life and death. Morale in the 73rd Wing suffered.

A radical change of tactics was introduced by General Curtis LeMay when, on the night of March 9, 1945, he sent his B-29s to Tokyo at altitudes between five and eight thousand feet. Carrying no ammunition and with bomb bays full of incendiaries, around three hundred B-29s droned through the darkness over the target. Aided by gusty conditions down below, the Superfortresses' fiery cargo gutted over fifteen square miles of Japan's first city.

To capitalize on the surprise factor of the tactical change, LeMay scheduled five missions in ten days. The "fire blitz" taxed air and ground crews and their B-29s to the limit, but they performed magnificently and Japan's fate was sealed.

A third wing, the 313th, had reached the Marianas, and their B-29s were involved in possibly the most effective B-29 mission - the aerial mining of Japanese ports and shipping lanes. Contributing also to the maximum efforts against the Japanese cities, the 313th's mining efforts were considered secondary at the time. The operation received little recognition until later analysis showed it to have been devastatingly effective - the enemy was literally being starved by the mining blockade.

The 314th Wing had begun operations from Guam in February, and the 58th Wing left India and moved up to the Marianas in late spring of 1945. They flew their first mission from Tinian on May 5, and with his four wings of B-29s LeMay was able to put up to five hundred Superfortresses over Japan. The war dragged on, but Japan was obviously finished - it was only a matter of time.

A fifth B-29 wing, the 315th, flew its first mission on June 26, 1945. The 315th was equipped with specially modified Bell B-29s, armed only with a radar-controlled tail turret and fitted with "Eagle" radar. Their specific mission was the destruction of the Japanese petroleum industry, and although the strategic importance of their strikes was diminished by the fact that the industry was already in a critical state, the experiment with "Eagle" was highly successful.

Probably the most historic missions of the B-29's war were flown by one squadron, the 393rd Squadron of the 509th Composite Group. Their fifteen B-29s arrived on Tinian in June, and on August 6 and 9 they dropped two atomic bombs on Japan. The war ended within days, and the Japanese surrender is often linked with the disasters which befell Hiroshima and Nagasaki. However, the relative effects of the various B-29 campaigns - the incendiary attacks on the cities, large and small, the aerial mining, the destruction of strategic targets, the atomic bombs - are impossible to gauge. Cumulatively, the operations of the B-29s brought Japan to its knees without an invasion, and did it in the space of fourteen months. The "billion dollar gamble" had paid off.

The 498th Group's Torchy, 42-24646 (right), taking off from Isley Field on Saipan (above). This airplane was so badly damaged later on the April 13 Tokyo mission that she was patched up and returned to the States as war weary. (Thomas C. Griffin/Ed Prunuske)

Armorers work on The Heat's On, 42-24605, prior to the first Tokyo mission in November 1944. This airplane did not survive the early operations from the Marianas, and ditched following fuel transfer problems on December 27, 1944. Only four of the eleven crew were rescued. (Merle Olmsted)

When the 73rd Wing moved to Saipan late in 1944, they were subjected to numerous small enemy air attacks. While they were more a nuisance than a threat, they were costly. This 499th Group B-29, 42-65220, was damaged on November 27, 1944. (Richard M. Morgan)

After the early failure of high altitude precision bombing, the B-29s rained fire on Japan in a way unheard of in warfare. These are aimable incendiary clusters of M-69s, jellied-oil napalm bombs which put the major cities of Japan to the torch. (Morgan)

The 6th Group in formation. In the foreground is Snugglebunny, 44-69667, a group original which survived the war and went on to fly many more mission in Korea with the 98th Bomb Group. (Roberts)

The 6th's White Mistress, after veering off the runway on Tinian. This B-29, 42-24776, went overseas with the group and flew again after this incident. (Gahagan)

B-29s from the 9th Bomb Group, 313th Wing. (Carpi)

There were always exceptions to the rules...instead of carrying the letter 'W' in the circle on her tail, this 505th Group was given an inverted 'M'. (Don Roberts)

As the pace of B-29 operations was stepped up, there was little time to apply markings before or between missions. These two 9th Group aircraft, in various stages or markings, are headed for Tokyo in February 1945. The aircraft in the background is 42-63561, *Ready Teddy*. (John Swihart)

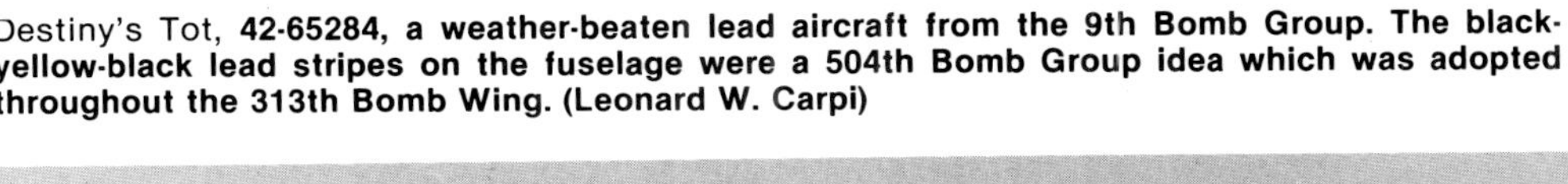
Destiny's Tot, 42-65284, a weather-beaten lead aircraft from the 9th Bomb Group. The black-yellow-black lead stripes on the fuselage were a 504th Bomb Group idea which was adopted throughout the 313th Bomb Wing. (Leonard W. Carpi)

(Top) The 6th Group's 42-94042, Myas' Dragon. **(John Gahagan)**

At the war's end, the 6th Group began painting the last four numerals of airplane serial numbers in tall black numbers on the dorsal fin. This is 44-70124, Tojo's Nightmare. **(Gahagan)**

A ground crewman fills the 85 gallon oil tank on the number two engine of the 468th's Hap Characters, **42-63424. The filler necks of the oil tanks were located at the side to make it impossible to overfill the tanks, and to leave enough air space to allow for expansion. (Tolzmann)**

B-29s used in Stateside training carried fairly uncomplicated unit markings. This B-29, being used for training by the 330th Group, carries the individual aircraft letter 'Q' in a black square. Other aircraft of the unit used other letters of the alphabet. (Ken Hurley)

When the 58th Wing's markings were changed in the Marianas, traces of older markings remained on many aircraft. The 462nd, however, was allowed to retain its red rudders after the group commander made a personal request to General Curtis LeMay. (Gahagan)

Some of the older B-29s were stripped and used in a variety of roles, including the 444th Group's *Bachelor Quarters*, 42-24507. The old airplane had amassed a total of 23 Hump flights and 32 missions, a proud record. (Wayne Floyd)

Hun-Da-Gee, 44-61546, flew with the 444th Bomb Group. (Larry Redmond)

The 29th Bomb Group's *Fire Bug*, 42-63566, taxies out from North Field, Guam, in April 1945. (USAF)

The 29th's Group 42-94034, with her shackled bomb load of MA7A2 jellied-oil incendiaries, each capable of spreading a forty-yard sheet of flame. (USAF)

Incendiaries

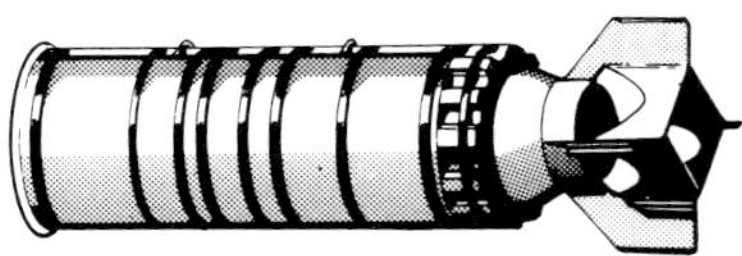

M69

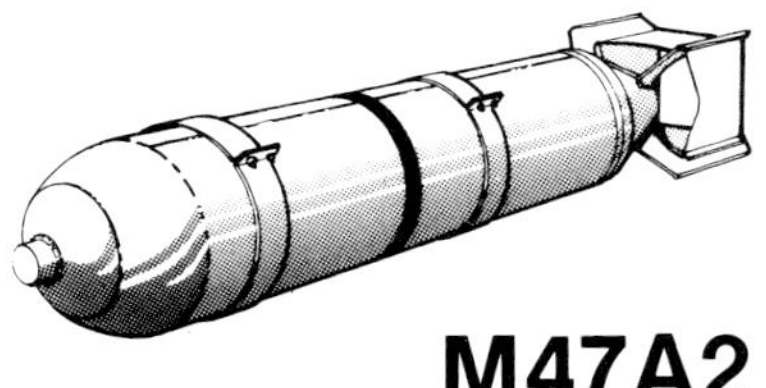

M47A2

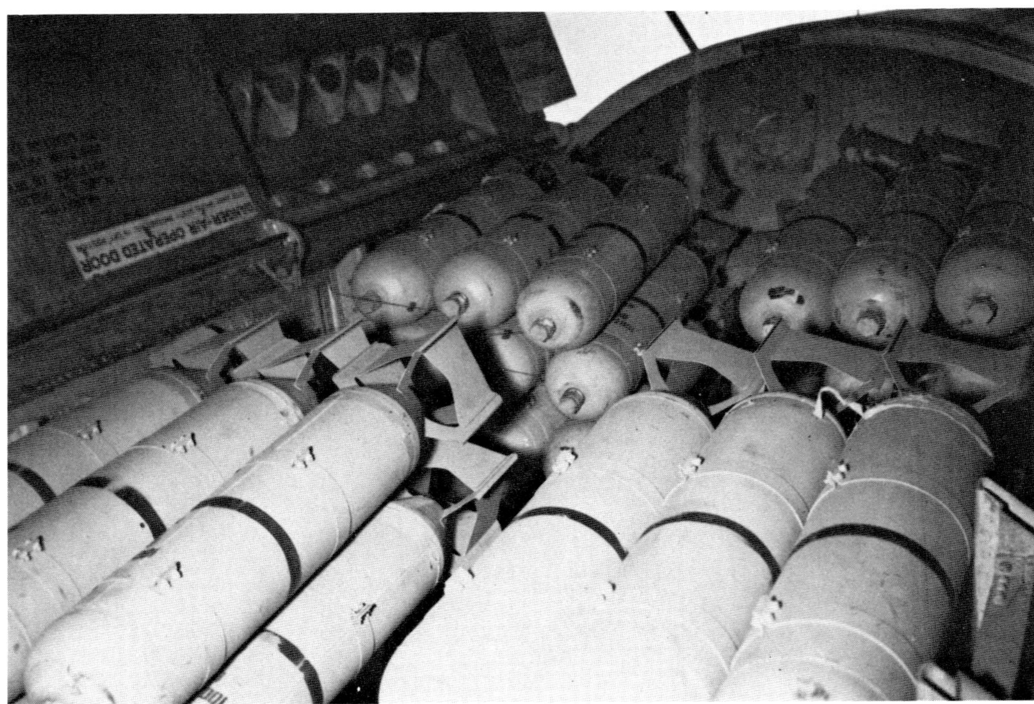

The 29th's formation heads out from Guam. (Eldon Elliott)

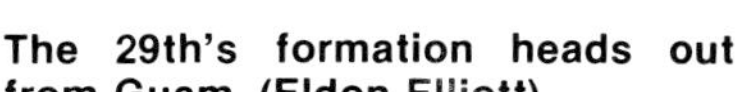

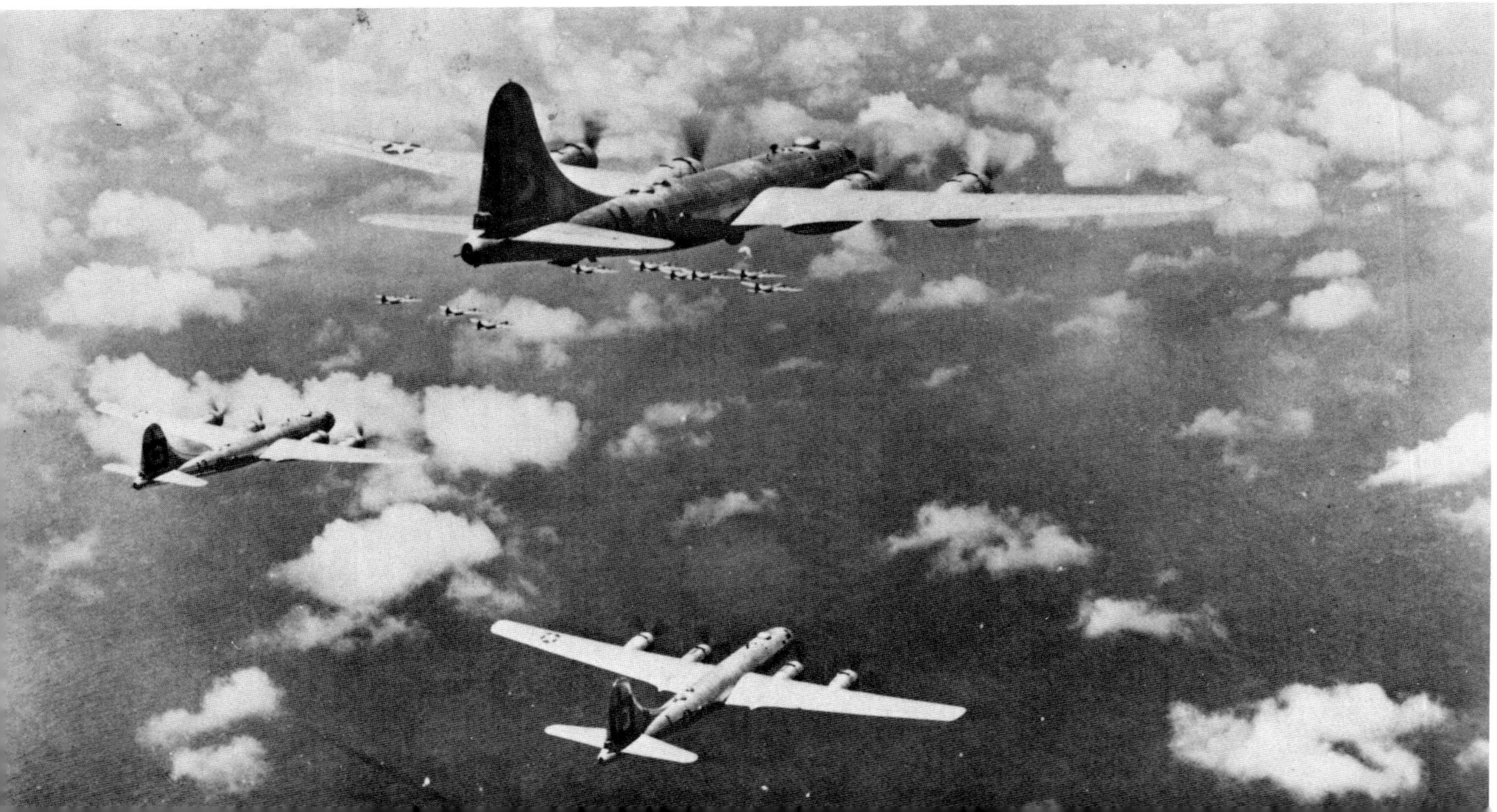

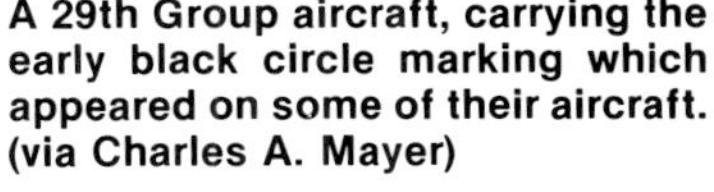

A 29th Group aircraft, carrying the early black circle marking which appeared on some of their aircraft. (via Charles A. Mayer)

This B-29, cracked up on landing, went overseas with the 29th Bomb Group. Initially she carried a large black circle on her tail, then the group marking of a black square with the white letter 'o' was applied. Her serial number, 42-24917, was applied in small numerals on the dorsal fin, and her group identification is repeated on the cowls of the outboard engines. On the left side of her nose is the nickname Nipp On Ese, while on the right side the nose is decorated with the 314th Wing "city" motif, and the name City of Oklahoma City. (Gahagan)

(Bottom left) Lord's Prayer, 44-69914, flew with the 314th Wing's 39th Bomb Group. (USAF)

For some reason, perhaps simply to provide at least some group identification during the remove-and-repaint operation, portions or even all of early markings were sometimes retained in addition to the new marking. This is the 497th Group's famous Thumper, 42-24623. (USAF)

The Cannuck, **42-24668, was a 500th Group original airplane which survived the war. The broad fuselage band is green, but, as in the case of several very late-war markings, its significance is not definately known. (Ray Pritchard)**

The 498th Group's Little Butch, **42-94014, with other members of the 873rd Bomb Squadron, at the coast of Japan. Below her is T-6,** Lucky 'Leven, **with traces of the early 73rd Wing tail markings still faintly visible. (USAF)**

A stripped B-29B, with 'Eagle' radar and a radar-equipped tail turret. The aircraft is 44-83944 of the 331st Bomb Group. (Clyde Matteson)

(Bottom) During the last weeks of the war the B-29s were being painted black on all undersurfaces, a proven defense against searchlights. This 498th Group aircraft is a Renton B-29A, 42-94046. (Thomas C. Griffin)

Inside the B-29

The Superfortress usually carried a crew of eleven men for its primary mission. Although it was the largest production airplane built up to that time, the B-29 was cramped when ready for war.

Six men were in the forward pressurized section: up forward in the nose was the bombardier with his bombsight, gunsight, table and control panel. Behind him were the two pilots with their controls and instruments. The flight engineer sat on the right side of the fuselage, facing aft, behind the pilots. Further back on the right was the radio operator with all his equipment, and the navigator was on the left. The interior of the B-29 was a maze of cables, oxygen lines and other equipment...the well of the upper forward turret took up so much space that the navigator's table had to hinged to allow people to move easily around it.

Back through the tunnel across the bomb bays were the gunners in the pressurized center section. The right and left blister gunners manned their pedestal sights on each side, while the Central Fire Control gunner sat in the "barber chair", a swivel-type stool below his top sighting blister. His gun sight was fitted with hand grips and was on a ring mount. The radar section was a windowless compartment aft of the three gunners.

The tail turret area was small, the pressurized section only yielding enough space for the gunner who occupied it. Even in the rear unpressurized section there was the auxiliary power unit, the well of the lower aft turret, and the ammunition cans for the tail guns. There was no space to spare on the B-29.

The view from the cockpit of a 505th Group B-29 as she moves toward the flight line on Tinian. (Roberts)

(Below right) Lieutenant Ed Porada of the 500th Group in the pilot's seat. (Porada)

Co-pilot Lieutenant John Swihart at the controls of the 9th Group's Ready Teddy. **(Swihart)**

(Above) The co-pilot's instrument panel. (Air Force Museum)

(Above left) The pilot's instrument panel on B-29 42-24583. (AFM)

(Left) The flight engineer's instrument panel; he handled most of the power plant, electrical and basic mechanical operations. (AFM)

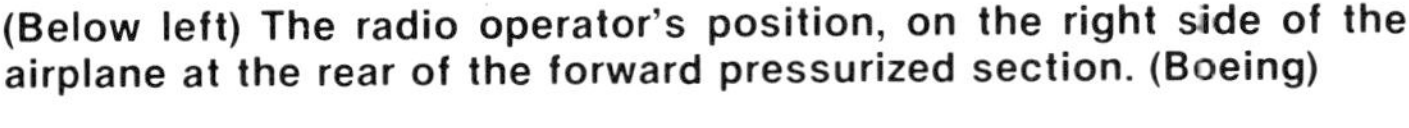

(Below left) The radio operator's position, on the right side of the airplane at the rear of the forward pressurized section. (Boeing)

(Below) The navigator sat opposite the radio operator. (AFM)

The four-gun upper forward turret on the 2nd Bomb Group's *Bad Penny*. Early B-29s had only two guns in this turret, but concern over the possibility of head-on fighter attacks led to this modification. (USAF)

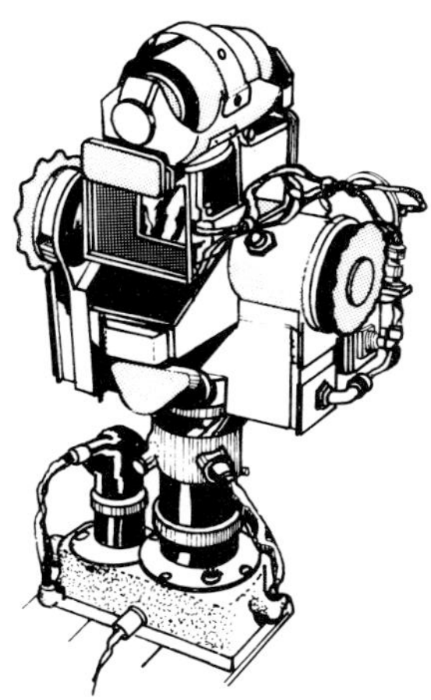

Gunner's Sight

(Below right) The left blister gunner operating his sight. (Boeing)

The right and left blister gunners used these pedestal sights, while the Central Fire Control gunner had a sight on a ring mount, and sat on a swivel-type stool beneath his top sighting blister.

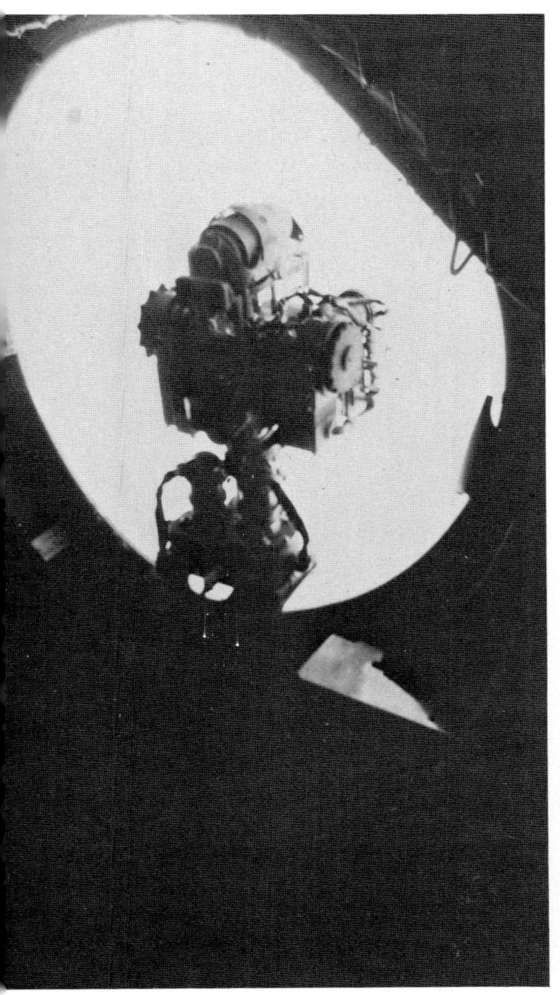

Tail armament on cannon-equipped B-29s looked menacing, but the 20mm gun jammed readily, was heavy, and had a slow rate of fire and a different trajectory from that of the 50-caliber machine guns. (Boeing)

(Below left) The tail turret on B-29A 42-93853. The 20mm cannon was later eliminated after it proved of little value in combat. (Boeing)

The 444th Group's Fu-kemal, 42-6352, an early Wichita B-29, after removal of the tail cannon. (Francis J. Johnston)

This streamlined top turret, the same as that used on the B-50, was fitted to the last production B-29s, built at Renton in 1946. (Gordon S. Williams)

The upper rear turret had provision for 500 rounds of ammunition per gun. The Central Fire Control gunner had primary control of this turret and secondary control of the upper forward turret. (Boeing)

The lower forward turret, primary control of which was held by the bombardier, who had a pedestal gun sight at his station in the nose. (Boeing)

Iwo Jima

The volcanic outcropping named Iwo Jima lay roughtly halfway between the Marianas and Japan, and the costly invasion of this island was undertaken because of its potential value to the 20th Air Force.

The capture of Iwo would allow friendly fighters to escort the B-29s to Japan, allow B-29s to fly a more direct route to Empire targets, provide a staging base for extremely long range missions, yield a base for air-sea rescue units, protect the Marianas from any sneak attack and, primarily, provide a haven for B-29s in trouble.

Iwo was invaded by the Marines on February 19, 1945, and in the bloody battle that followed over four and a half thousand Americans died. The ugly little island paid its first dividend just under two weeks later when Lieutenant Raymond Malo brought his 9th Group Superfortress in for the first B-29 emergency landing.

While its value as a fighter base was lessened by the inability of Japanese fighter defenses to impede the B-29s, its value as an emergency base was indisputable. By war's end nearly two and a half thousand B-29s had touched down there under emergency conditions. The biggest single influx of the giant bombers occurred during the night of June 8, 1945, when over one hundred Superforts dropped out of the dark skies.

The first B-29 to land on Iwo Jima was the 9th Group's 42-65286, commanded by Lieutenant Raymond Malo. It landed on the embattled island on March 4, 1945, and took off again about two hours later. (USAF)

Although its most important contribution was as an emergency haven for B-29s in trouble, ugly little Iwo Jima served several purposes. It was a base for escort fighters, a staging base, and a base for rescue planes. (USMC)

The 500th Group's Ramblin Roscoe, **42-24664, had two engines shot up by a fighter over Tokyo on April 15. The main gear tires were also damaged. She made a night landing on Iwo and crashed into this embankment. (USAF)**

Hard landing: this B-29's skin was rippled from nose to tail by the violence of her arrival, but she got her crew safely to Iwo. (Larry Reineke)

Caught both ways: this 505th Group B-29 was over Iwo with a windmilling propeller on #3 engine, which flew off, knocking out the #4 engine and tearing this huge hole in the fuselage. The airplane went out of control and crashed into another Superfort's tail, smashing the nose and demolishing the top turret. Nobody was seriously hurt. (USAF)

The 19th Group's 42-65342, broken up on Iwo in May 1945. (USAF)

Jo, 42-65337 of the 444th Group, collided with another B-29 over Tokyo and struggled back to Iwo. She was cannibalized for parts. (USAF)

This 462nd Group B-29 was one of the last to crack up on Iwo. (Morgan)

When the 313th Wing began flying long mining missions to seaports in Korea, Iwo was used as a staging base. Ground crewman are pulling the props through on the 6th Group's *Reamatroid*, 44-69672. (Larry Reineke)

The 6th Group prepares to take off on a mining mission from Iwo Jima in July 1945. *Myas' Dragon* heads the lineup. (Reineke)

The Photo Superforts

The photo recon version of the Superfortress, the F-13, was designed by the Air Technical Service Command in conjunction with Boeing and the Fairchild corporation.

The first F-13 conversion was a Wichita airplane, 42-6412, and eventually a total of 118 Wichita and Renton B-29s were modified.

The F-13s carried normal B-29 armament initially, and carried more cameras than any earlier reconnaissance aircraft. There was a trimetrogon arrangement - three K-17 cameras mounted side-by-side, one pointing straight down and the others flanking it and pointed toward the horizons - for photomapping territory. For post-mission and specific recon work there were two K-22 cameras in a split vertical mount, capable of covering areas about two miles wide from 20,000 feet. The sixth camera in the normal arrangement was a K-18, used for similar work to the K-22s, but covering a wider range and for close-ups of specific areas mapped by the trimetrogon.

Due to the extremely high altitudes flown by the F-13As, the camera windows were made of 3/4" thick glass which could withstand the pressure differences, and fitting these windows involved considerable structural work on the airframe. This was carried out by Continental Airlines at the Denver Modification Center.

The F-13A was designed by the Air Technical Service Command in conjunction with Boeing and Fairchild, and the modifications were made to the airplanes at Continental's Denver Modification Center. The three large glass cutouts in the underside of the airplane were for vertical, trimetrogon, and split vertical installations of cameras. (AFM)

The camera windows on each side of the fuselage were for the trimetrogon arrangement of cameras, used primarily for mapping purposes and taking three overlapping photographs simultaneously. (AFM)

F-13As were conversions of Wichita and Renton B-29s, and went into combat with Flight "C" of the 1st Photo Squadron from Hsinching, China. This is the third Wichita photo plane, 42-24567. (U.S. Army)

The most famous photo Superfort of all was Tokyo Rose, **42-93852, which photographed Tokyo prior to the first mission from the Marianas in November 1944. (USAF)**

Yokohama Yo-Yo, **42-24621, coming in to land. (John H. Mitchell)**

Giving F-13As names which were synonymous with their roles was an obvious but pleasant pastime. The 3rd Photo Squadron's *Double Exposure*, 42-24877, carried artwork based on a Varga painting from *Esquire*. Other F-13As like *Dark Slide* and *Under-Exposed* had similarly interesting artwork. (Bob Watson)

(Bottom) In June 1945 *Yokohama Yo-Yo* was flown home by the squadron commander, Colonel Patrick McCarthy, and placed on exhibition in conjunction with a War Bond Drive. The 3rd Photo Squadron's F-13As were identified by a black letter 'F' on the nose and tail, and later a black tail tip was added. (USAF)

Double Exposure and *Yokohama Yo-Yo*. The cost of converting a B-29 to an F-13A ran to about $400,000. (Mitchell)

Radar

All combat B-29s were equipped with radar, and while there were problems with the use of some of the equipment there was also a consistent improvement in the performance of both equipment and operators during the course of the B-29's war.

The basic radar equipment of the Superfortress was the AN/APQ-13 ground scanning radar, developed by the Radiation Laboratory at M.I.T. in conjunction with Bell Telephone and Western Electric. The APQ-13 scanner revolved and swept through 360 degrees, and was housed in a variety of radomes situated between bomb bays. Initially these radomes were partially retractable, but ultimately a streamlined, aerodynamically superior tear-drop unit was designed at the Denver Modification Center.

Early 58th Wing B-29s, (and some later aircraft operating in specialized roles) were equipped with the Philco SCR-729 airborne interrogator, and all B-29s carried SCR-695 "Identification, Friend or Foe" (IFF) equipment.

The 315th Wing's modified B-29s were fitted with AN/APQ-7 "Eagle" radar, with the antenna housed in an airfoil under the fuselage. The antenna swept from side to side through sixty degrees, the beam being concentrated in the forward path of the aircraft. A much higher frequency was used, yielding a clearer radar scope presentation of images. The 315th Wing B-29s were also fitted with the AN/APQ-15 tail turret, with a short-range radar designed by General Electric. The unit was light and fairly simple, with a range of about two thousand yards, all that was required of it.

Combat B-29s had provision for the easy field installation of various radar countermeasures equipment. A number of semicylinder "cans" were fitted at locations around the fuselage, with coaxial cables leading from them to the radar compartment. Antennas could thus be quickly and easily fitted without disturbing the skin or pressurization of the aircraft - a cover plate was simply removed. Higher frequency antennas, not aerodynamically clean, were usually covered with plastic teardrop shapes.

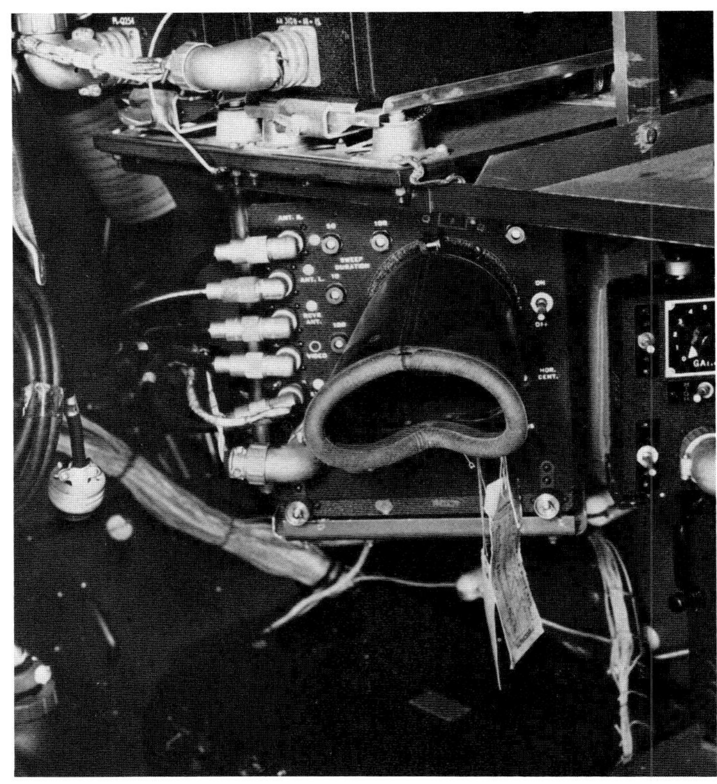

The SCR-729 was fitted at the radio operator's position. The equipment was originally intended to serve the same purpose as ground radar, identifying friend or foe. The SCR-729 was able to challenge other aircraft, sending out an interrogating pulse. (AFM)

Early 58th Wing aircraft were equipped with the SCR-729 interrogator, which measured range and bearing to other aircraft. The old 444th Group B-29 Hore-Zontal Dream **carries the distinctive antenna used with this equipment. (Olmsted)**

All combat B-29s carried APQ-13 radar, but three different randomes were used to house it. This 39th Group airplane, City of Albuquerque, **has her radome retracted. (via Tom Young)**

This 330th Group B-29, 44-69790, has the later APQ-13 radome, a teardrop streamlined unit designed by the Denver Modification Center. (Edwin D. Wolf)

This view of the "Eagle" radar antenna shows the airfoil shape and the fit between the open bomb bay doors. (AFM)

A Bell B-29B with the APQ-7 'Eagle' antenna mounted in an eighteen foot airfoil section beneath the fuselage. This airplane is 42-63672. (AFM)

APQ-7 'Eagle' Radar

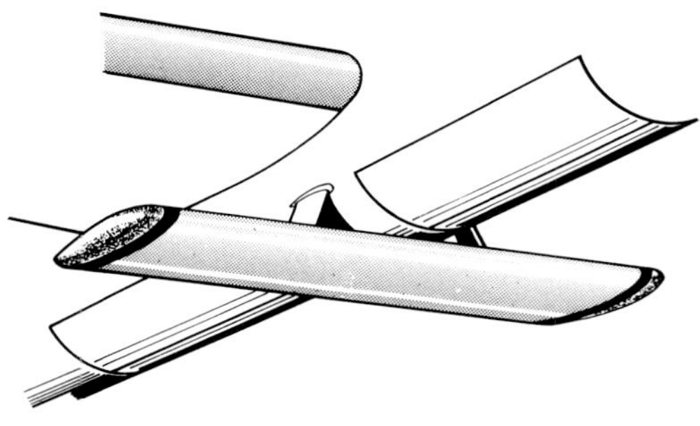

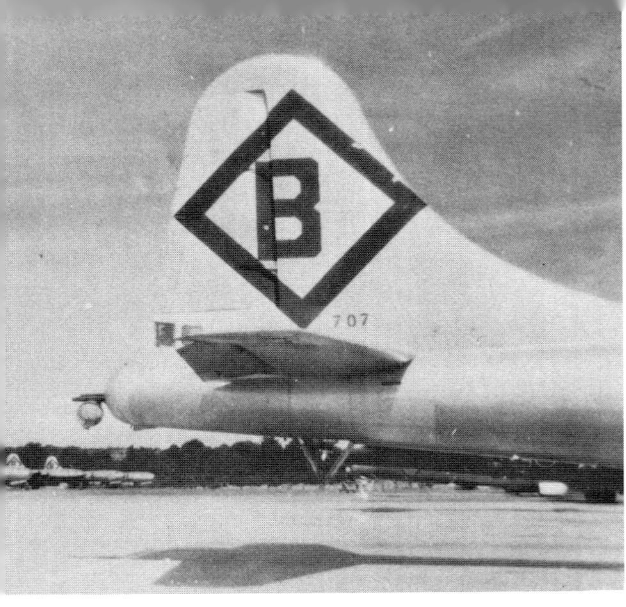

The APG-15 on the 16th Group's 42-63707. Although the radar tail turret hardly received a thorough combat testing, it caused problems and was generally considered a failure. (Desmond Mock)

The APG-15 tail turret installation on a 331st Group B-29B. (Matteson)

When losses and damage to B-29s began to creep up, radar countermeasures activity was increased. This is a "Porcupine" from the 6th Bomb Group, named obviously for the profusion of antennas which identified these aircraft. "Porcupines" carried sixteen to twenty jamming sets and two specialist operators. (Roberts)

The final radome was this aerodynamically superior installation on the last batches of B-29As, built at the Renton plant. It probably houses APQ-23 radar, a development of the APQ-13. (Boeing)

Unit Insignia

While all B-29s in the 20th Air Force were identified by large tail markings, individual groups and squadrons often used more personal motifs. There was no hard and fast rule, and these markings were sometimes used in conjunction with them.

In the 58th Wing the 462nd Bomb Group developed their "Hellbirds" motif as a result of a design competition held within the group late in 1944. The distinctive design was ultimately carried on the right side of the nose of all 462nd Group aircraft. The 468th Group had two distinctive emblems - the shooting star design on the nose, which usually incorporated any nickname, and the Billy Mitchell flag, painted on the tail. The 40th Group's airplanes were beginning to carry the emblem "Kagu Tsuchi" - Scourge of the Fire God" towards the end of the war. The 444th Group's B-29s consistently carried their squadron insignia on both sides of the nose, throughout the war.

On Saipan the 73rd Wing's B-29s usually carried only unit markings, although squadron insignia have been recorded on the noses of 497th Group B-29s, and the 874th Squadron of the 498th Group used an official squadron emblem designed for them by B. E. Hogarth. When the order came to remove the nose art, the 73rd Wing devised a wing insignia, a black winged ball with a yellow barb in which names could be lettered.

Tinian's 313th Wing developed individual group markings with a fairly common theme, although there were differences. The 6th Group carried its insignia on both sides of the nose, usually with a red and white streamer trailing aft from it. Within the streamer were painted nicknames, if any, in red. Late in the war, the 9th Group was apparently carrying the group emblem on the right side of the nose with a white streamer. The 504th had devised a black ball with a winged golden hammer and a yellow streamer, but it was apparently not widely used by war's end. The 505th had several aircraft with squadron emblems and a green and white streamer, similar in style to that used by the 6th Group. The true consistency of these markings is in the colors dominating the streamers - red was the 6th Group's color, white for the 9th, yellow for the 504th, and green for the 505th, and these colors were also, of course, carried on their tail tips and cowlings.

The 314th Wing devised its own symbol, and it was administered at wing level. While the left side of the nose of B-29s in this wing were allowed to carry an "unofficial" name, the right side was usually used for a "city" name. This scheme was perhaps initiated to gain press coverage for the plane and crew in the city of its name, and this was often the case; some of the crews also expected a hearty civic welcome and free liquor when they got home. Although the choice was nearly unlimited, one 330th Group B-29 became **Quaker-City** because **City of Philadelphia** had already been claimed by another group. The emblem used by the 314th was a map of North America in a blue circle, with a pennant carrying the name.

Snuffy, **42-24873, from the 444th Bomb Group. She carries the 676th Squadron insignia, a bomb-hurling version of Walt Disney's Reluctant Dragon. (John W. McKenna)**

The 874th Squadron of the 498th Bomb Group had this squadron insignia, a green dragon head, designed for them before they left for the Marianas. It appeared on both sides of the noses of their original aircraft. Fay **is 42-65210, lost on March 24, 1945. (Edward G. Prunuske)**

The 468th Group had two distinctive motifs...their shooting star nose design, and the General Billy Mitchell flag on their tails. The flag had been designed by the controversial airman and used aboard his yacht. (Pidhayny)

Captain Charles Besore's Grider Gal, **42-24884, with the 6th Bomb Group's distinctive marking. The bust of pirate Jean Lafitte harked back to the group's long service in the Panama Canal Zone in the early 1920s and 1930s. Aircraft nicknames were painted in a red and white streamer behind this group insignia, but no other form of artwork was permitted. Toward the very end of the war, the other three groups in the 313th Wing were developing similar insignia motifs. (via John Dulin)**

The four groups of the 314th Wing adopted this motif - a map of North America with a pennant carrying the name of a chosen city. This is the 29th Group's City of Arcadia, **42-93925. (Chuck Hawks)**

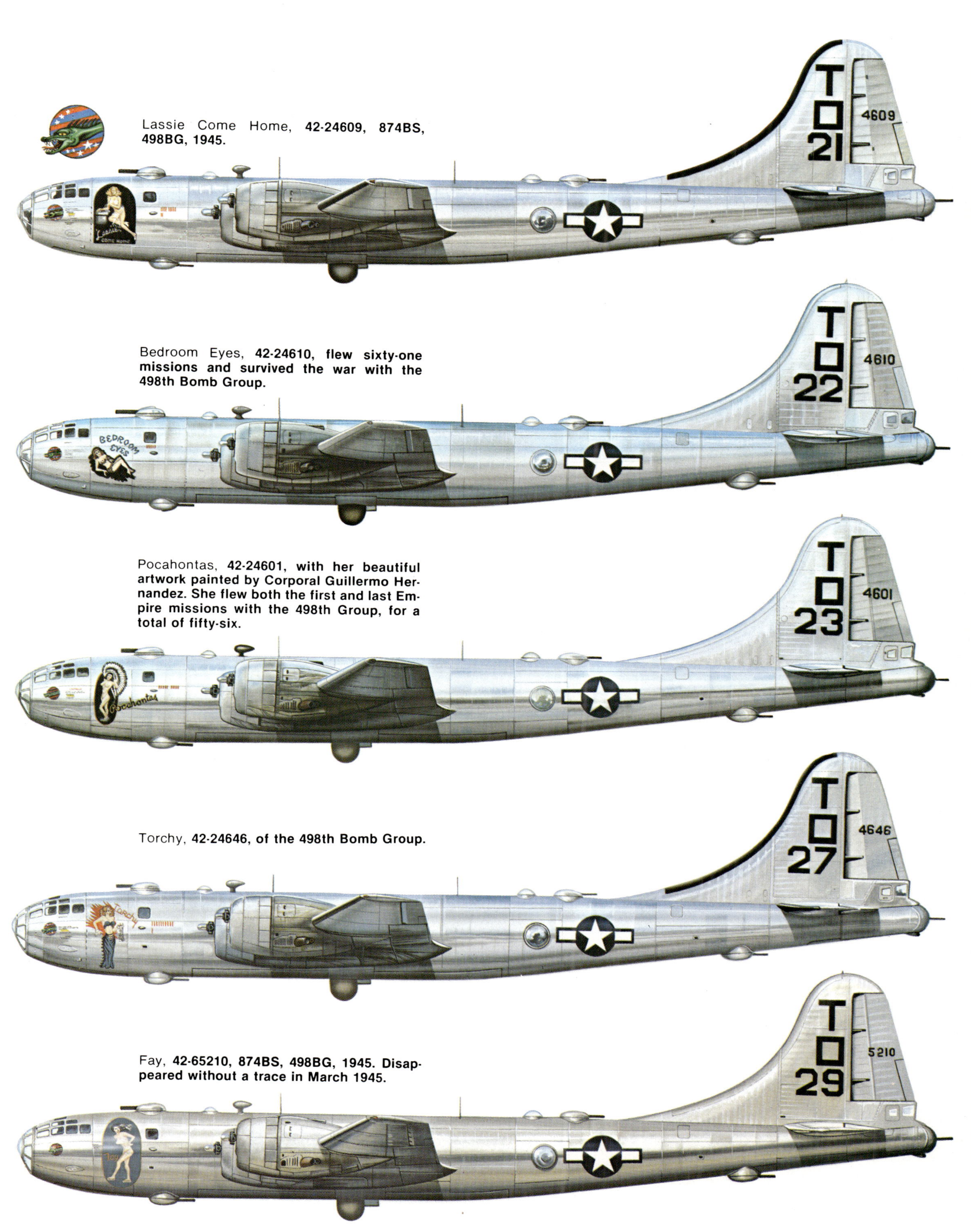

Lassie Come Home, **42-24609, 874BS, 498BG, 1945.**

Bedroom Eyes, **42-24610, flew sixty-one missions and survived the war with the 498th Bomb Group.**

Pocahontas, **42-24601, with her beautiful artwork painted by Corporal Guillermo Hernandez. She flew both the first and last Empire missions with the 498th Group, for a total of fifty-six.**

Torchy, **42-24646, of the 498th Bomb Group.**

Fay, **42-65210, 874BS, 498BG, 1945. Disappeared without a trace in March 1945.**

Mission Symbols

Inventiveness did not end with nose art and nicknames, and while the traditional recording of an aircraft's career in red or black stencils of bombs was used in all B-29 wings, there were interesting variations on the theme. The F-13As used a camera lens silhouette to record their operations, mining missions were recorded in a variety of styles, and there were symbols for PW Supply missions such as pack mules, symbols for weather recon flights and fighter navigation missions. Sometimes there were stars above bomb stencils, or purple hearts to record crew injuries. There were sinking Japanese ships, and airplane silhouettes or flags to symbolise fighter claims. There were highly individual mission symbols, such as those carried by the 497th Group's **Thumper.** In the 462nd Group a special symbol was approved for recording "Superdumbo" rescue flights - a red silhouette of the Disney flying elephant - but apparently it was not used before the war ended.

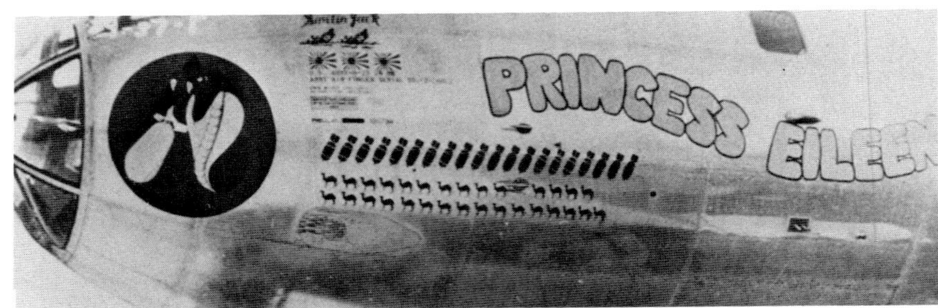

The 444th Group's Princess Eileen, **42-24462, displays typical 58th Wing mission symbols - a couple of sinking Japanese ships, three Japanese flags for fighters shot down, twenty bomb stencils and thirty camels for flights over the Hump. (Smith)**

When three F-13As were loaned to 13th Air Force for a series of missions from Morotai, the camera lens stencils were painted in red; since the missions were flown over Java, a little white coffee pot was included in those symbols on Double Exposure. (Barry Gilkes)

Symbols for mining missions flown by the 313th Wing varied - the six punctuating the normal bombing stencils on the 9th Group's Ready Teddy **are one verson. (Swihart)**

Dearly Beloved, 44-70069, with nine milk bottle symbols in addition to her twenty-four bomb stencils. (Gahagan)

The telephone poles painted on 42-24728 from the 462nd Group are unique, and tell a story - heading out from China on the way to the Marianas, the bomb bay doors of this airplane flipped open at 300 feet altitude. The B-29 mushed and dropped to the ground, mowing down eight telephone poles. Luckily the pilots were able to get her down safely, and the damage was repaired. (Clay Sandhofer)

Aircraft from the atom bombing 509th Composite Group decorated their specially modified B-29s with "fat man" symbols, the name given to the plutonium bomb which was dropped on Nagasaki. (via John Dulin)

Holley Hawk was from the 58th Bomb Wing. (Teed)
The 468th Bomb Group's Bella Bortion, 42-63355. The dark blue rudder bands identify her as a 793rd Squadron aircraft. (USAF)

A formation of the 9th Group B-29s, with white cowl bands and tail tips. (Malayney)

Later in the war, the 9th Bomb Group began painting the group insignia on the forward starboard side of the fuselage. Most WW2 B-29 crews used the port side of the fuselage for personal nose art, so the group insignia could be placed without interfering with the aircraft name.

Esso Express, 42-6242, a tanker from the 468th Bomb Group.

The Big Time Operator, 42-24791, of the 9th Bomb Group.

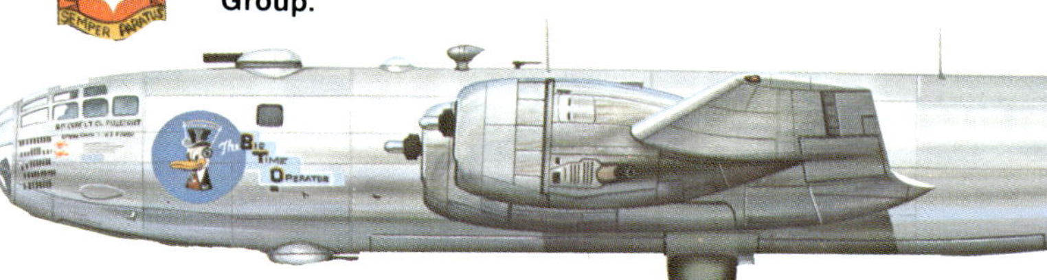

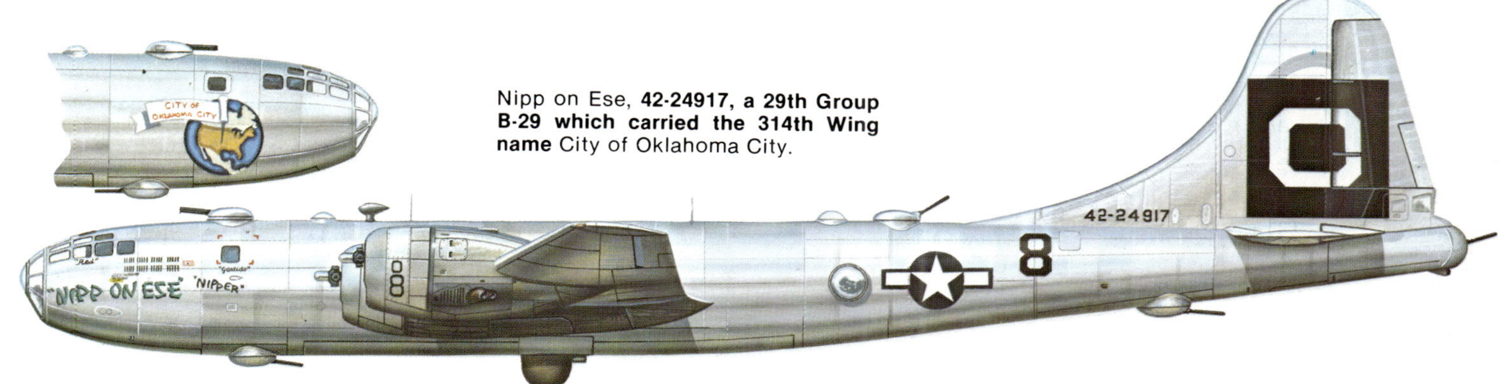

Nipp on Ese, **42-24917, a 29th Group B-29 which carried the 314th Wing name** City of Oklahoma City.

The 462nd Group, Colonel Alfred Kalberer's "Hellbirds", were identified by their red rudders. The 462nd was one of the four original B-29 groups which moved to the Marianas from India. (R. Wallace Teed)

Walt Disney's Thumper is usually associated with the famous 497th Group aircraft of that name, but this 504th Group B-29 on Tinian also carried it. (Malayney)

Destiny's Tots, **42-65293, flew with the 497th Bomb Group from Saipan. The mission symbols below the cockpit are in the form of diapers. (Donnelly)**

The 497th Group's Thumper, **42-24623. Each mission was recorded in the form of a miniature rabbit, with the target noted on the bombs and any fighter credits in the form of Japanese flags. (Donnelly)**

Captain Bill Lind's Star Duster, **42-93858 from the 870th Squadron of the 497th Group. (Donnelly)**

The Atom Bombers

Colonel Paul Tibbets' 509th Composite Group had a brief but momentous combat career. Flying specially modified Martin-built B-29s, with fuel injection engines and Curtiss reversible pitch propellers, and stripped of all but the tail armament, they dropped the atom bombs on Hiroshima and Nagasaki. The group's fifteen B-29s were in the 393rd Squadron, and when they arrived on Tinian they carried the unit's distinctive marking, a black arrowhead in a circle. This was soon replaced by spurious markings - 497th Group insignia, a large "A", was applied to aircraft 71, 72, 73 and 84. Airplanes 77, 85, 86 and 88 carried 444th Group markings, including the colored belly band; numbers 82, 89, 90 and 91 carried 6th Group tail insignia; and the final three aircraft, 83, 94 and 95 bore the 39th Group's tail marking.

The aircraft were still easily identifiable - the phony 497th and 444th markings were applied in a rather less exact way than in the actual groups, and the stripped B-29s carried individual airplane numbers in a far higher range than normal bomber units.

The 393rd Squadron B-29s were:

No.	Serial	Name	Nominal Aircraft Commander
71	44-27303	**Jabbitt III**	Capt. John Wilson
72	44-27302	**Top Secret**	Lt. Charles McKnight
73	44-27300	**Strange Cargo**	Lt. Joseph Westover
77	44-27297	**Bockscar**	Capt. Frederick Bock
82	44-86292	**Enola Gay**	Capt. Robert Lewis/Col. Paul Tibbets
83	44-27298	**Full House**	Capt. Ralph Taylor
84	44-27296		Capt. James Price
85	44-27301	**Straight Flush**	Capt. Claude Eatherly
86	44-27299	**Next Objective**	Lt. Ralph DeVore
88	44-27304		Capt. George Marquardt
89	44-27353	**The Great Artiste**	Lt. Charles Albury/Maj. Charles Sweeney
90	44-27354		
91	44-27291	**Necessary Evil**	Lt. Norman Ray
94	44-27346		Lt. Col. Thomas Classen
95	44-86347	**Laggin' Dragon**	Capt. Edward Costello

NOTE Some of the aircraft nicknames in the 393rd Squadron were not applied until after the atomic bombing missions.

Major Claude Eatherly's Straight Flush, **44-27301, stripped of all but the tail armament and bearing false 444th Group markings. (via John Dulin)**

The 509th Group's special B-29s were fitted with Curtiss reversible-pitch propellers, with cuffs to assist cooling. Here the ground crew is pulling the props. This was done to drain out oil that collected in the lower cylinders, thereby preventing damage to the engines when they were started. (Dulin)

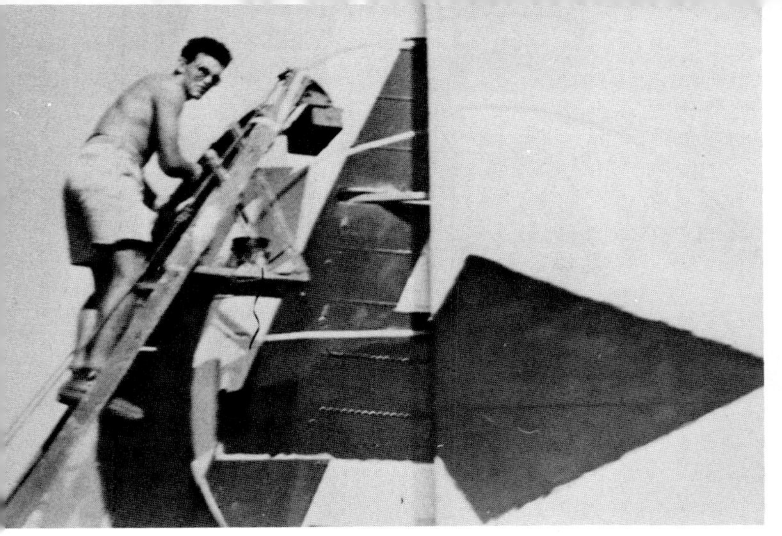

Repainting the 509th's distinctive arrow tail marking on Strange Cargo. **(Dulin)**

Lt. Joseph Westover's Strange Cargo. **(Dulin)**

Lt. Ralph DeVore's Next Objective **was one of four 509th B-29s carrying 444th Group markings to disguise her mission.** (via **John Dulin)**

Co-pilot Fred Olivi leans from the window of The Great Artiste. **The first four "fat man" symbols below the window are for missions using 'pumpkins' - five-ton high explosive bombs which the 509th used during the build-up to the atomic bomb missions. (Olivi)**

The 498th Bomb Group's Lucky 'Leven, 42-24695, which flew sixty missions and survived the war. Her crew chose the name after an earlier close shave, and it proved to be the right one. (Edward T. Donnelly)

A 9th Group lead airplane, with the black and yellow fuselage bands which were developed by the 313th Wing. On her nose is the insignia of a naval construction Seabee unit. (Malayney)

The Great Artiste from the 509th Composite Group. The first four black "fat man" symbols below the window are for missions using "pumpkins", five-ton high explosive bombs which the unit used during the buildup to the atomic missions. The fifth and sixth symbols, in red, denote the Hiroshima and Nagasaki strikes. (Teed)

Miss Judy, 44-61555, reached the 462nd Group on Tinian in June 1945. (Teed)

The 504th Group's Dina Might, 42-65280, after her pinup girl artwork had been removed from the nose. (Teed)

Untouchable, 42-24506, of the 462nd Bomb Group.

Fire Belle, 44-61653, of the 444th Bomb Group.

44-62260, of the 581st Air Resupply and Communications Squadron.

The 28th Squadron's No Sweat **crashlanded at a fighter base in Korea, and was then demolished by a P-51 which suffered engine failure on takeoff and crashed into her. (Amthor)**

Southern Comfort, **44-61749, crashed and burned in Japan in November 1950. (Amthor)**

Jita, **a subtler version of "Jab In The Ass", with the red nose band of the 19th's 93rd Squadron. (Amthor)**

The 93rd Squadron's Hot To Go, **on Okinawa in 1951. (Amthor)**

The 19th's Stateside Reject **crashed and burned on Okinawa in November 1950. (Amthor)**

Art Gallery

The names and nose art painted on the B-29s provided a glimpse of humanity in an inhuman situation. Around March 1945, all the artwork was ordered removed from the aircraft noses, an action variously credited to pressure from the Red Cross, chaplains, and women's groups back home. To some this meant very little, but others felt the names were important, a lucky charm. There was always a preference for the Rabelaisian in the names and paintings, although they ranged from the patriotic to the blatantly sexual. They ran the whole gamut of plays on words, vulgar expressions, song titles, hometown names, movie titles. They featured movie stars, pin-up girls, comic strip characters, politicians, generals. Often there was a subtle twist. The art itself ranged from the highly professional to the enthusiastically amateurish.

The artwork on airplane noses reflected a youthful exuberance which was soon lost in the battle zone. None of it ended up in art galleries or museums; too much of it ended up twisted, broken and burned somewhere in Japan, at the bottom of the sea, or in some forgotton rice paddy in China.

Artwork on the early 58th Wing B-29s was widespread, but the most elaborate and inventive paintings appeared on 462nd Group aircraft. Hull's Angel, **42-63362, was named for her pilot, Captain Carl Hull.** Mysterious Mistress, **42-6312, was possibly inspired by the delights of Cairo, where the B-29s stopped over on their long journey to war. (Seely)**

Supine Sue, **42-24653, was the first 500th Group B-29 to arrive on Saipan, and flew over forty missions. (Morgan)**

Peace on Earth, **42-63412, was one of several 497th Bomb Group aircraft with paintings by John G. Albright. (Charles Russo)**

Another lucky B-29 was the 498th Group's Tanaka Termite, **42-24749, which flew sixty missions. (Prunuske)**

Whether Commanding General of the Army Air Forces'Hap' Arnold would have approved of this use of the air force insignia and his name is debatable. The airplane is the 497th Group's 42-24774. (Watson)

The symbol of the 20th Air Force appeared on a few B-29s, including the 500th Group's 20th Century Sweetheart. **(Morgan)**

Top of the Mark, **with art by Dick Thompson, was named for the San Francisco night club. The story goes that any crew member was entitled to free drinks there. (Amthor)**

Hanna-Barbera's cat decorated the 19th's Atomic Tom. **(Lynch)**

Bug's Ball Buster, **44-61638, carried on the distinguished war record of the Warner Brothers rabbit. (Lynch)**

Probably every group in two wars had an Our Gal **- this one was in the 19th Group on Okinawa (Amthor)**

Spirit of Freeport, **44-62060, of the 22nd Bomb Group, Korean War.**

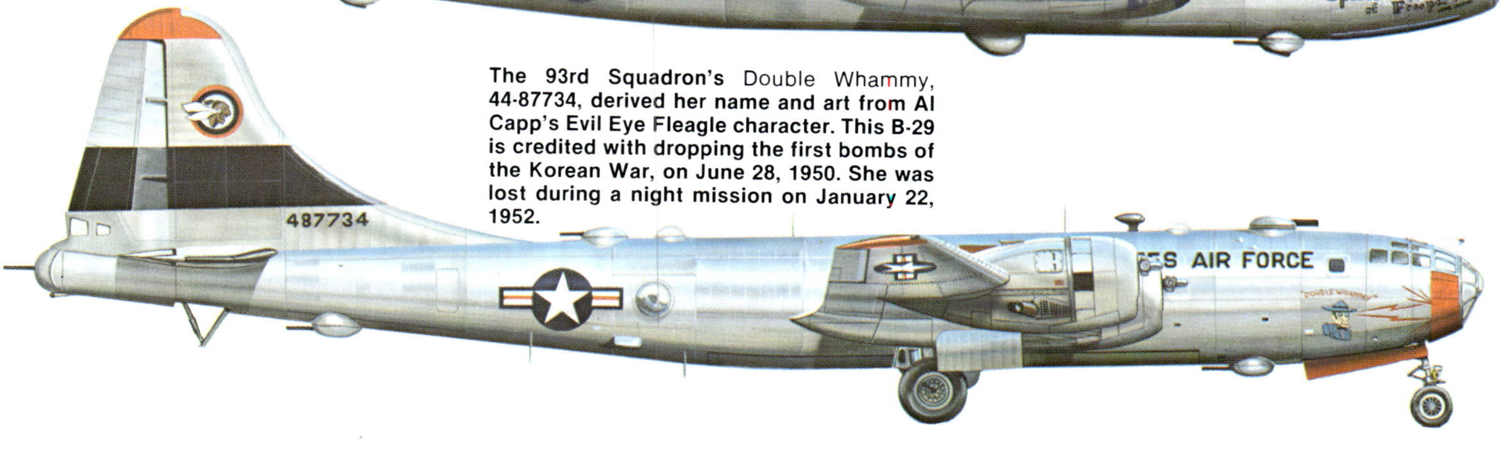

The 93rd Squadron's Double Whammy, **44-87734, derived her name and art from Al Capp's Evil Eye Fleagle character. This B-29 is credited with dropping the first bombs of the Korean War, on June 28, 1950. She was lost during a night mission on January 22, 1952.**

Rock Happy, **44-62053, of the 93BS, 19BG, Korea.**

Never Hoppen, **44-61562, flew over 80 missions with the 28BS, 19BG in Korea.**

Miss Fortune, **of the 19th Group's 28th Squadron. (Amthor)**

Purple Shaft, **42-65361, serving with the 19th Bomb Group's 30th Squadron during the Korean War. (George Amthor)**

Miss N.C., **44-68376, had artwork painted by a 19th Group airman named K. Walter. (Amthor)**

Four-A-Breast, **44-86323, survived the Korean War with the 19th Group. (Amthor)**

Persuade-her, **from the 19th's 28th Bomb Squadron (Jim Lynch)**

The F-13As carried some of the most professional artwork, a typical being the 3rd Photo's *Poison Ivy*, 42-24585. The airplane's name derived from that of the crew chief, Sergeant Ivey. (Watson)

Several B-29s were decorated with quite elaborate caricatures of their own crews. *Pappy's Pullman* flew with the 504th Group from Tinian, and *Waddy's Wagon* was the 497th Group's 42-24598. (Carpi/Morgan)

The variety of nose art was stunning, and Varga's *Esquire* masterpieces were often copied almost exactly. However, the accompanying verses by Phil Stack were usually passed over -but not on the 500th Group's 42-24643. After all the effort, this airplane deserved to survive, and did. (Morgan)

Nose art often appeared on both sides of the nose, and there were always minor variations. *Constant Nymph*, 42-63487, was painted by a 500th Group draftsman, Corporal Henry Johnson, and his skill led to the almost perfect duplication of the insignia on each side of the nose. (via Charles A. Mayer/Reineke)

The 19th Group's Lucifer, 45-21745, one of three B-29s specially modified to carry the huge Tarzon bombs. There were extensive revisions to the bomb bay and bomb bay doors, and the radar was moved forward, replacing the lower forward gun turret. The aircraft were also fitted with B-50 nosepieces to give bombardiers better visibility. On the left side of her nose Lucifer carries six symbols for the missions flown with the smaller Razon bombs, and ten symbols for Tarzons.

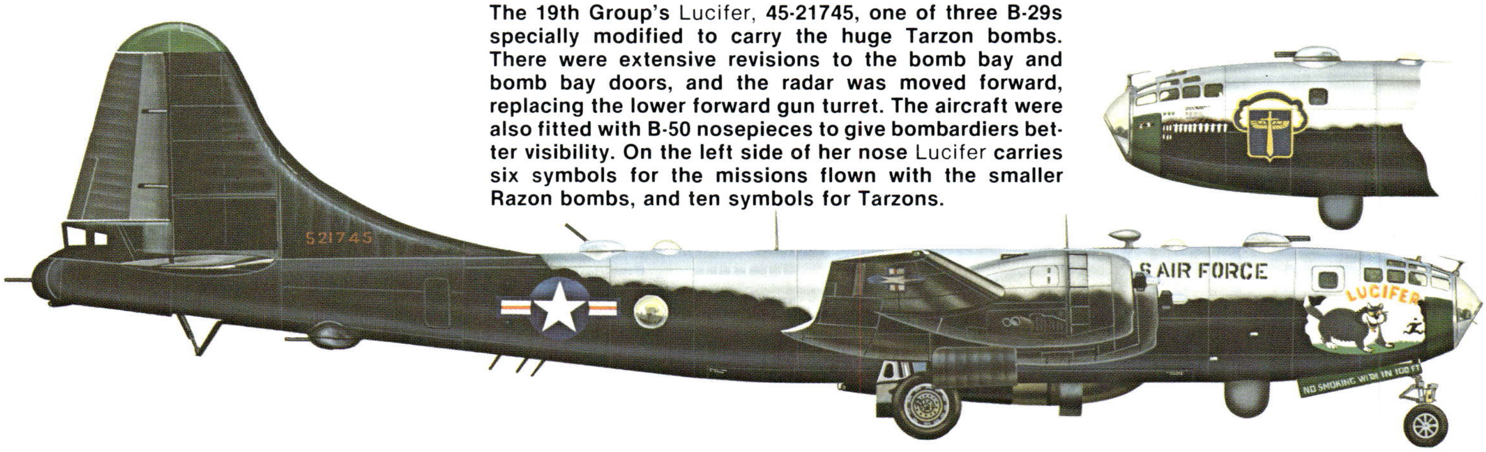

The 30th Bomb Squadron's Bluetailfly, 42-65272, was the first B-29 in the Far East to complete 100 combat missions. By the time Captain Vito Fierro took her home in 1952 her grand total was 142. The 30th Squadron's insignia, a cop twirling his nightstick, was particularly appropriate in the so-called "police action" in Korea. The 19th Group insignia was carried on the left side of the nose of all their B-29s.

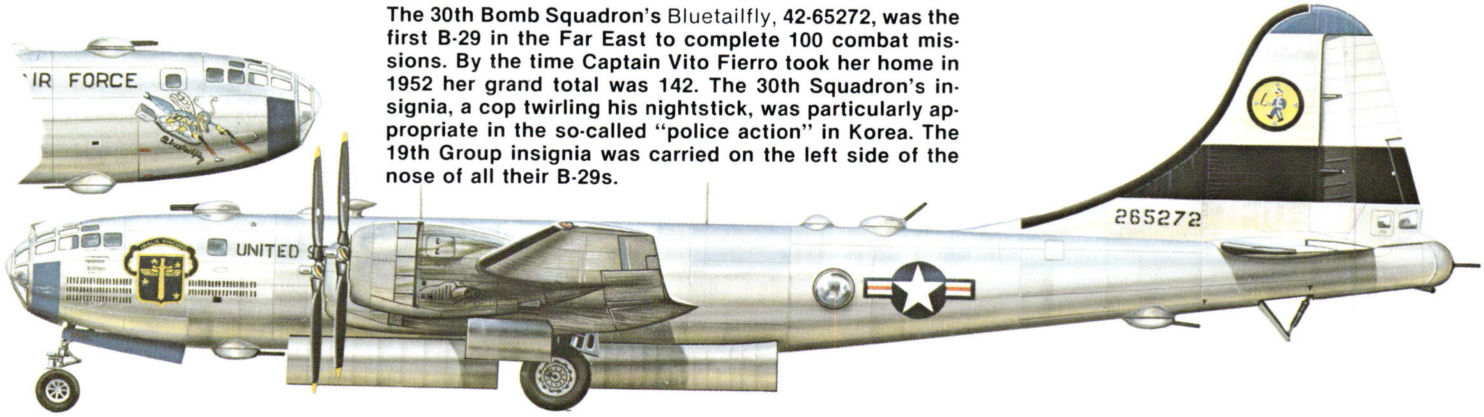

The 92nd Group used this map of Korea on the left nose of their B-29s. When the 92nd went home, this B-29, 44-61830, was passed on to the 19th. (Amthor)

The most inventive nose artwork in the 19th Group appeared on B-29s from the 93rd Squadron as on "Max Effort". (Amthor)

While most of the artwork in the 19th Group was fairly typical, there were clever exceptions. Dead Jug was a cryptic reference to the still troublesome R-3350 engine. (Amthor)

This garish piece of art, by Walter, has a story behind it. The airplane, 44-87661, was orginally the 468th Group's American Beauty III during World War II, and she still bears part of her old group markings. The plane was later named Ugly, then finally Koza Kid, an insulting comment on the ladies of an Okinawan village near the 19th Group's base. (Amthor)

Seabees decorated many of the early 313th Wing aircraft on Tinian, adding their own unit insignia to the airplanes in more than a dozen cases. Indian Maid, 42-24806, flew with the 504th Bomb Group. (Ed Hering)

The 9th Group's Goin' Jessie, 42-24856, dropped the two-millionth ton of bombs in World War II. (Carpi)

Flag Ship, 42-63504, was from the 504th Group, and was the first of their B-29s to reach the Marianas. In addition to the caricatures of the crew members, by their positions, she carried a Seabee insignia. (Reineke)

Slick's Chicks, **42-24784, was elaborately decorated, with numerous pieces of artwork, but the paint hardly had time to dry - she was lost on the 505th Group's second Empire mission on February 10, 1945. (Carpi/Hering)**

Seabee insignia on the 505th Group's 42-24815. (Hering)

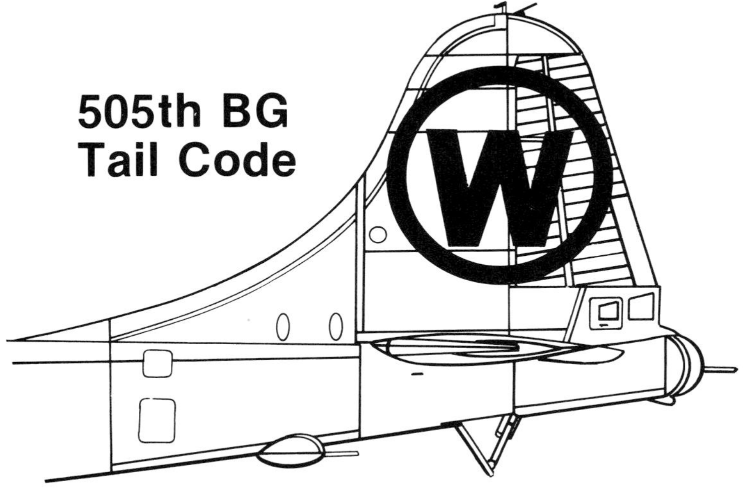

Hometowns were remembered in some B-29 names, like the 504th's Bainbridge Belle. **(Carpi)**

Artwork knew no bounds on the B-29s, until the order came to remove it around the spring of 1945. By then the 504th's The Life of Riley, **42-65241, was lying at the bottom of the Pacific Ocean, a casualty of a March 1945 mission. (Carpi)**

The One You Love, **44-69727, served with the 504th Group during World War II then went back to war again with the 98th Group in Korea as** Hot't Trot. **(Carpi)**

Walt Disney's creations appeared on very few B-29s, most crews preferring hotter-blooded themes. Donald Duck made it on the 9th Group's 42-24791, The Big Time Operator. **This airplane went overseas with the 9th and flew a total of forty-eight bombing and mining missions, an outstanding record. (Gahagan)**

Long John Silver was a classic and obvious enough name for a gleaming B-29, and appeared on the 462nd Group's 42-63502. (L. J. Arents)

Milt Caniff's Miss Lace was always a popular motif, appearing in most groups. The 468th's version appeared on 44-87658, and the 498th's Miss Lace was 42-63554 - she flew 49 consecutive missions without an abort and served on Saipan until the end of the war. (Dave Vincent/Morgan)

Artwork survived in the 58th Wing's 444th Group, and appeared on most of their B-29s. This is Ho-Hum, **44-70123. (Redmond)**

A popular pinup adorned the 497th's Teaser, **42-63526. She was lost on March 25, 1945. (Watson)**

Although running a poor second to nude beauties, comic characters were a popular basis for B-29 art. Red Hot Rider, **42-65338, is from the 497th Bomb Group. (Watson)**

Plays on words don't come any easier than this one, *Tinny-Ann.* **She flew with the 6th Group. (Dick Snodgrass)**

The 462nd Group always had some of the most inventive and unusual artwork, such as *Phony Express.* **(Arents)**

Lady in Waiting **also served as** *Shaft Absorber,* **using the same piece of artwork on the nose. (Hitchcock via Olmsted)**

The Record Breakers

When the war ended, an impressive series of B-29 record flights began almost immediately. A few weeks after the war, 20th Air Force received orders to make a non-stop flight with three B-29s from Japan to Washington. Each airplane carried a twelve-man crew and 10,000 gallons of fuel, and while the flight had to stop over at Chicago before reaching their goal, the planes had carried out the first non-stop flight from Japan to the United States. Within three weeks, General Frank Armstrong in **Fluffy Fuzz IV** led four B-29s nonstop from Japan to Washington in twenty-seven hours. The climax of the distance flights came on November 20, 1945, when Colonel "Bill" Irvine set a new world nonstop record by flying the B-29B **Dreamboat** from Guam to Washington, a distance of 8,198 miles. Their B-29 had been lightened down to 66,000 pounds empty weight, but gross weight at takeoff from Guam was 151,000 pounds - the fuel-laden B-29 was indicating 145 miles an hour before the runway ended and she took to the air. Soon after, Irvine flew the airplane from Burbank to New York to set a new transcontinental record, averaging 451.9 miles per hour. Irvine flew **The Challenger** from Long Beach to Oahu, then in March 1946 took **Fluffy Fuzz V** from Honolulu to Manila nonstop. Irvine said the record, 21 hours and 49 minutes, was "accidental", as it was a routine flight.

Back on Guam, Irvine directed ground operations for the "Marathon Project" during May 1946, and the following records were achieved: **The Challenger** was flown to 41,561 feet true altitude with a 10,000kg load, and to 39,520 feet with 15,000kg. A B-29 named **Queen of the Neches,** 44-84065, carried 2,000kg to 46,522 feet on May 13 then the following day took 5,000kg to 45,252 feet. **Fluffy Fuzz IV** made 47,910 feet carrying 1,000kg.

In October Irvine was breaking records again. With **Pacusan Dreamboat,** (the old **Dreamboat** with further modifications), grossing 149,000 pounds and carrying 13,400 gallons of fuel, Irvine took off from Honolulu and flew 10,000 miles over the Arctic to Cairo, Egypt in 39 hours and 36 minutes.

A few weeks after the war ended, 20th Air Force received orders to make a non-stop flight with three B-29s from Japan to Washington. Four B-29s were selected, stripped of armament, polished and waxed. Their group markings were completely removed and the 20th Air Force insignia painted on their tails. One aircraft was a stand-by, and the others were numbered 1, 2 and 3. Each was commanded by a general and crewed by veterans. This is the lead plane, commanded by General Barney Giles; General Curtis LeMay was in #2; General "Rosie" O'Donnell flew #3. A fuel shortage in Giles' airplane caused all three to land at Chicago. (J. Ivan Potts)

The B-29B Pacusan Dreamboat, **44-84061, was involved in several record flights. Virtually a flying gas tank, this airplane, commanded by Colonel "Bill" Irvine, flew nonstop from Honolulu to Cairo in thirty-nine hours. They took off from Hawaii with a gross weight of 149,000 pounds, including 13,400 gallons of gasoline. (Boeing)**

The Challenger, **42-63731, was involved in the "Marathon Project". In May 1946 this B-29B carried a 10,999kg load to a true altitude of 41,561 feet. (Boeing)**

Operation Crossroads

Approved by President Truman in early January 1946, Crossroads was a gigantic peacetime exercise involving the effort of nearly 42,000 people. Its objective was to study closely the nuclear effect of two atomic bombs, one of them to be dropped from a B-29.

When the planning for Crossroads began, it was obvious that the 509th Group was the only unit capable of dropping the bomb. The Army Air Forces element of the operation was known as Task Group 1.5, made up of about two thousand personnel drawn largely from SAC and under the command of General Roger Ramey. This Task Group was responsible for delivering the bomb and providing aircraft to photograph the explosion and gather scientific data. The Task Group moved to Kwajalein in March 1946, and flew dress rehearsels in preparation for the "Able Day" missions.

On July 1, Able Day, five "Silverplates" - the name for the B-29s modified to carry atomic bombs - participated with one standard B-29 and eight F-13As. The bomb carrier was 44-27354, **Dave's Dream**, with **Top Secret** and a companion B-29 in the recon role. The sixth B-29 was the command aircraft. **Dave's Dream** dropped a Fat Man-type bomb on seventy-three ships lying off Bikini, sinking five and badly damaging nine.

Task Group 1.5 also participated in the second phase of Crossroads, an underwater explosion several weeks later, by providing numerous aircraft for photographic, data collection and support functions.

Enola Gay, **still commanded by Colonel Paul Tibbets, was to drop the Bikini bomb, but a mechanical failure led to the substitution of** Dave's Dream. **(USAF)**

Air Weather Service sent three of their RB-29s for Crossroads, as Task Group 1.57 Air Weather. This B-29, Warm Front, **44-62128, flew directly over Bikini sending back continuous weather observations prior to the first test on July 1, 1946. (Boeing)**

Crossroads markings were simple...bombers carried a large 'B' in a black square, photo planes an 'F', weather planes a 'W', and blast gauge aircraft simply retained their normal 509th markings, the arrowhead in a circle. Sweet 'n Lola, **44-61578, flew on Able Day. (Pete Bowers)**

Strategic Air Command

SAC was created on March 21, 1946 as one of the three major combat commands of the USAAF. The backbone of the new force was the B-29, but at the end of the year SAC had only nine B-29 groups, and only six of these had aircraft. The groups were the 7th, 28th, 43rd, 97th, 307th, and 509th. There was also the 16th Photo Recon Squadron with F-13As.

In October 1946 the 28th Bomb Group went to Alaska for six months of Arctic training, the first SAC group to leave the continental United States. Late the following month the B-29s were used as a diplomatic tool when, after a couple of American C-47s were shot down over Yugoslavia, six 43rd Group B-29s flew to Germany and patrolled the border of Soviet territory.

SAC's B-29s rotated to Yokota, Japan, and flew mass simulated raids on American cities as part of the readiness program over the following year. SAC began receiving B-36s and B-50s in 1948, and the B-29s found themselves redesignated "Medium Bombers". During the Berlin crisis the B-29s were again called to flex their muscles - one 301st Group squadron was at Furstenfeldbruck in Germany, and the other two were moved to Goose Bay, Labrador, to be ready for immediate movement to Europe. The 307th and 28th Groups were also alerted, and moved to bases in England during July, 1948.

SAC's Superfortress strength peaked during 1948, and the B-29 was the front-line bomber during the Korean War. However, it was only a matter of time before newer types took its place. At the end of June 1957 there were only sixty Superfortresses in Strategic Air Command, all of them KB-29 tankers.

The 43rd Bomb Group was equipped with the last thirty B-29As, including this one, 44-62310. The 43rd identified its squadrons by the use of colored tail tips, nosewheel doors, fuselage bands and cowl sections. The colors were yellow and black stripe for the 63rd Squadron, blue for the 64th, and red for the 65th. (Gordon S. Williams)

The Berlin blockade in June 1948 led to the removal of SAC B-29s from Germany to England. 44-62328 is a 307th Group B-29A, at Lakenheath RAF Station. (USAF)

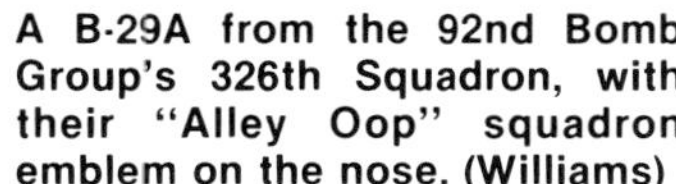
A B-29A from the 92nd Bomb Group's 326th Squadron, with their "Alley Oop" squadron emblem on the nose. (Williams)

In 1948 the photo recon versions of the Superfortress were redesignated RB-29As. This one, 45-21846, has non-standard modifications and carries the markings of the 90th Strategic Reconnaissance Wing. (Williams)

The Weather Watchers

Weather had played a major role in the way the war against Japan had been fought, and in 1945 bomb groups began carrying certain B-29s as "special weather aircraft" in their records. Even so, Air Weather Service did not receive the 53rd, 54th, 55th, and 59th Reconnaissance Squadrons until March 1946, and two of these, the 54th and 55th, were "paper" organizations.

On May 25, 1946, Air Weather Service's first B-29 mission was flown from Castle Air Force Base. During that year some B-29s were modified for the weather role, in two basic configurations - weather recce RB-29s stripped of armament, and one squadron, the 54th, with combat-capable aircraft. The major changes, aside from the armament, were the installation of unique meteorological equipment, such as the aerograph for measuring temperature and relative humidity, the psychrometer for measuring water vapor content and radio and radar altimeters.

Once transition was made into RB-29s, the 53rd Squadron moved to Bermuda, the 54th to Guam, the 59th to Alaska; the 55th, based in California, handled Stateside weather requirements.

The first flight over the top of a hurricane was made by an AWS B-29 on October 7, 1946, and on March 17, 1947 the first AWS RB-29 flight over the North Pole was made. In September 1949 the West was able to confirm that Russia had detonated its first atom bomb, when an AWS Superfort from Guam discovered the nuclear debris.

A weather B-29 crew usually consisted of nine men - two pilots, navigator, weather observer, radio operator, flight engineer, radar observer and left and right scanners.

In November 1949 all B-29s were grounded until their engines could be replaced, and the B-29s were showing signs of age. Many of the Air Weather Service aircraft has over 1,000 hours on the airframes, and these were usually rugged hours, involving many descents and climbs, with corresponding changes in throttle settings, fuel flow, engine temperature, oil pressure and so on. The long missions were flown through heavy weather, with turbulence, icing and storms a regular part of the flights.

Because of AW's relatively low priority, a replacement for the B-29s was unlikely, so a program was begun to modernize them, and it took nearly two years to complete. The designation WB-29 came into use in August 1950.

During the Korean War the 512th Recon Squadron (which became the 56th Strategic Reconnaissance Squadron (Medium, Weather) in February 1951), flew its first mission on June 26, 1950. A 512th B-29, with General O'Donnell aboard, led the initial strike into North Korean from Japan on July 13. Making daily flights over or near enemy territory, the 512th WB-29s were fitted with tail guns and transmitted the data they gathered in the clear, which was their best protection, as the information was valuable to the enemy. Flying a fixed track over Korea, they could have been shot down relatively easily. However, after June 9, 1952, the track was moved south of the 38th Parallel and the WB-29s never went north agains; they had by then flown around 750 combat missions.

Other weather B-29s played their role in Korea. Captain Charles Cloniger, in the 514th Squadron's **Typhoon Goon** from Guam, completed a typhoon recon mission in a WB-29 with one engine feathered on September 8, 1950; the data he was gathering on the typhoon's intensity and position was vital to the forces loading at Kobe for the Inchon invasion.

Air Weathers Service's peak B-29 strength was eighty, in 1954, tapering off until, in 1957, their last year of service, there were only two.

This WB-29, 42-65281, carries the dropsonde chamber and APQ-13 radar beneath the fuselage, and the "bug catcher" above - an air filter assembly used during nuclear sampling missions. (Air Weather Service)

(Below left) The weather observer and his equipment occupied the nose position in the WB-29. (AWS)

Weather aircraft flying over the North Pole from Alaska were suitably nicknamed -Lonesome Polecat **was 44-62151, from the 375th Recon Squadron. (AWS)**

Rescue

The Air Rescue Service was established in March 1946, but it was only by good luck that the SB-29 served in it, due to the airplane's heavy fuel consumption at a time of military austerity. The first two SB-29s were received in February 1947, equipped with the A-3 lifeboat. They carried search radar in place of the lower forward turret and the radio operator's position was moved from behind the upper forward turret to the waist of the airplane, across from the radar station. The normal SB-29 crew was eleven men, with two pilots, navigator, two flights engineers (one of them acting as nose scanner), two radio operators, two scanners in the waist and one in the tail, and a radar operator.

Air Rescue Service had a maximum strength of nineteen B-29s in 1952, but there were actually only sixteen conversions to SB-29s. The 10th Rescue Squadron in Alaska substituted teams of huskies for rescue missions over the ice pack.

During the war in Korea, when Communist night fighters threatened B-29 missions, 37th Air Rescue Squadron SB-29s from Komaki, Japan, flew long range rescue-escort missions for their sister aircraft: SB-29s trailed the last bomber of a stream then orbited at the ingress point to provide assistance on call when the bombers came back.

The sixteen SB-29 conversions were 44-61671, 44-69957, 44-69971, 44-70119, 44-84030, 44-84078, 44-84084, 44-84086, 44-84088, 44-84096, 44-84112, 44-86303, 44-86308, 44-87644, 44-87665 and 44-87761.

This underwing flare pod was installed on SB-29s of Flight "D", 11th Air Rescue Squadron, operating out of Andersen AFB, Guam. (Boeing)

The first A-3 lifeboat was fitted to SB-29 44-61671. The A-3 was all metal, with self-inflating chambers which righted the boat if rough water capsized it. (USAF)

One of the first B-29s assigned to Air Rescue Service, this aircraft was never modified to the SB-29 configuration. (William T. Larkins)

This SB-29, 44-84078, flew with the 3rd Rescue Squadron. Headquartered at Johnson Air Base in Japan, the 3rd had detachments at Yokota, Misawa and Ashiya. (USAF)

The B-29 Tankers

In 1948 a Boeing plant at Wichita was reopened to convert B-29s to tanker aircraft for Strategic Air Command. These first aircraft were designated KB-29Ms and employed a British-developed system of trailing hoses and grapnel hooks. To operate the first conversions, the 43rd and 509th Air Refueling Squadrons, the first such units in the USAF, were activated and assigned to the 43rd and 509th Groups respectively. A total of 92 KB-29Ms were produced, and the refueling system was quite a "Rube Goldberg" arrangement according to veterans of the early days. The tankers were equipped with two 2,500 gallon fuel tanks in the bomb bays and a large reel aft of the pressurized center section with about 200 feet of 3" wire-reinforced hose with a heavy brass nozzle. At the beginning of the operation, the tanker trailed a couple of hundred feet of cable line from the end of its hose and the receiver aircraft, (originally 74 B-29s modified at Wichita and dubbed B-29MRs, with a funnel-like receptacle in the tail just below the right elevator), trailed a contact line which fed from the center of the funnel and had a grapnel hook at the end. When the cables were out from both aircraft, they flew a crossover maneuver to engage the two lines, then held formation with the tanker above. The hose operator in the receiver hauled in its cable and removed the grapnel and then wound in the tanker's hauling line, which pulled the refueling hose off the tanker's reel and drew the nozzle into the receptacle where it was locked in place. The reel operator on the tanker opened the fuel valves when word was received that the nozzle was engaged.

A far better aerial refueling system was the Flying Boom, designed by Boeing and using a telescoping metal pipe to pass fuel from the tanker to the receiver under pressure. The boom was "flown" into contact with the receiving aircraft by using the control surfaces at the end of the boom. It was an indication that the Superfortress was nearing the end of its days that only one aircraft, 44-62205, designated an EB-29, was equipped as a boom receiver for test purposes. The first boom-equipped tanker was an EB-29, the others were KB-29Ps.

The boom was used to refuel jet fighters but was not as suitable for this purpose as a variation of the hose system employing a drogue, at the end of the hose, which engaged with a probe on the nose of the fighter. Some KB-29Ps were adapted for the new system by the installation of a short hose and drogue at the end of the boom. In all, 133 B-29s were converted to KB-29T tankers at Renton, and two YB-29Js were also fitted with the equipment and became YKB-29Js.

A unique tanker was the YKB-29T, an aircraft which was converted in England to a three-hose arrangement which could fuel three fighters simultaneously. One hose was in the tail, the other two were in pods under the wingtips.

KB-29Ms of the 43rd Air Refueling Squadron link up with 49th Fighter Wing Thunderjets over the Philippines. The F-84s were flying nonstop from southern Japan to Bangkok on a 2500 mile training flight in December 1953. The tail tips and belly bands on the tankers are blue with white diagonal stripes. (USAF)

KB-29M 44-27329, from the 421st Air Refueling Squadron. (USAF)

Airplanes refueling from tankers were aided by this series of indicator lights along the belly of the KB-29. They instructed the pilot to correct his position by colored lights and the words "right, left, up, down, forward and aft". (Boeing)

Boom-equipped KB-29Ps from the 509th Air Refueling Squadron taxi out at Hickam in October 1952, for the operations known as "Fox Peter Two". This was the 7,800 mile flight of seventy-five F-84Gs from Texas to Misawa Air Base in Japan. (Boeing)

KB-29Ps from the 91st Air Refueling Squadron, also involved in the "Fox Peter Two" flight. (Boeing)

91st Squadron KB-29Ps with F-84s from the 27th Fighter-Escort Wing. The jet fighters had to be refueled in a dive and even then they would usually stall off the boom when they were full. (Boeing)

Extra Duty

While the bulk of the B-29s spent their service lives in fairly "normal" pursuits, there were a number of interesting and relatively little-known uses of the Superforts.

One B-29, 45-21793, became **Ole Miss VI** with the All Weather Flying Center and was involved in cosmic ray research in South America in 1946.

The U.S. Navy gained four B-29s in 1947 and they were used as mother ships and test beds in a variety of projects. Another test-bed was 44-84043, used by General Electric to test turbojet engines - it was dubbed XB-29G. McDonnell used B-29 44-84111 to carry their tiny XF-85 "Goblin" parasite fighter.

Specially modified B-29s were used to test massive conventional bombs after the war in "Project Ruby", a joint American-British operation. This involved testing bombs like the 22,000-pound "Grand Slam" (so large that half of it was actually outside the B-29's modified bomb bays) against underground German structures which had proven immune during the war, such as the submarine assembly plant at Farge.

During the Korean War the 19th Bomb Group, in conjunction with Air Proving Ground teams, tested 1,000lb Razon radio-controlled bombs against bridges with some success. The 19th also combat-tested the big Tarzon, a six-ton weapon with a similar electronic guidance system. The Tarzon B-29s were specially modified and each squadron had one aircraft; the bombs were loaded over a pit. The use of Tarzons was suspended in August 1951 after the 19th Group's commander, Colonel Payne Jennings, was lost when attempting to jettison a Tarzon at low altitude prior to ditching. Investigation had revealed that the bomb could not be dropped "safe", as the tail assembly would pull off on impact and arm the bomb.

A more conventional use of the ageing B-29s was in the radar evaluation squadrons. Stripped of all armament and offensive equipment, the B-29 was an airplane which was "available." The initial radar calibration unit was at Langley, commencing in 1949. In the fall of 1950 the unit moved to Griffiss Air Force Base, and the B-29s were used to calibrate ground radar sites. Later they provided aircraft for fighter interceptor training and were involved in ECM training, detecting and jamming friendly radar. The Revron B-29s were designated TB-29, and an aircraft from the 6023rd Radar Evaluation Squadron actually made the last USAF B-29 flight, in June 1960.

Other TB-29s were used by Tow Target squadrons, and there were a number of miscellaneous B-29 versions, including the XB-44, 42-93845, used as a test bed for Pratt&Whitney engines, six B-29s winterized for Alaska and redesignated B-29Fs, the XB-29H used in armament tests, half a dozen aircraft fitted with fuel injection R-3350s and "Andy Gump" nacelles for service testing and called YB-29Js, there was the VB-29, 44-87755, a VIP transport used by the Third Air Division on Guam, and there was the XB-39, an old service test YB-29 fitted with Allison engines. Others were designated EB-29 and used in various equipment tests by the Wright Air Development Center.

One of the most intriguing B-29 operations was that of the Air Resupply and Communications squadrons. Their B-29s' only armament was the tail turret, there was provision for dropping parachutists where the lower aft turret had been, and the bomb bays were fitted with special racks for leaflet dropping. There were three of these squadrons, all formed at Mountain Home Air Force Base during 1951 and 1952. The squadrons were trained to operate from any altitude, and the 580th Squadron lost one of their aircraft one night in the North African desert, south of Tripoli, when it flew into sand dunes. The 581st Air Resupply and Communications Squadron went to the 13th Air Force as part of the 581st Psychological Warfare Wing, and one of their black B-29s was shot down over Manchuria on January 12, 1953. The USAF crew were tried as spies and released from prison in 1955, and one of the CIA men aboard was jailed for twenty years. The third of these clandestine squadrons was the 582nd, which operated from Molesworth to England.

Andy Gump was an early Wichita B-29 used to test the modified nacelles which were to be fitted to later B-29As. The tall tail was to have been fitted to the B-29D, which was redesignated B-50. (Boeing)

This B-29-97-BW, 45-21748, was used at Eglin AFB, Florida to test the radio-guided "Tarzon" bomb, later used by aircraft of the 19th Bomb Group in Korea. (USAF)

B-29s were used in several test programs. This EB-29, 45-21800, was used by Bell to test both the XS-1 and X-1B (Boeing)

B-29 44-62093 was involved in the first wingtip-to-wingtip hook up of fighter and bomber aircraft. (USAF)

The Royal Air Force received 87 Superfortresses as a stopgap force between its old Lincolns and the jet Valiants. WF491 was originally 44-62198, and flew with 149 Squadron. RAF B-29s were named Washingtons. (Jeff Brown)

Stripped down and designated TB-29s, Superfortresses began going to radar evaluation squadrons in the late 1940s. The 1st Radar Calibration Squadron, later the 4713th Radar Evaluation Squadron, named their B-29s after characters from Snow White. This is *Dopey*, 44-70016. (USAF)

As the end drew near, TB-29s were used in inglorious roles. 44-87761 was assigned to Alaskan Air Command's 15th Tow Target Squadron, but was in such a weary condition that little or no use was made of it. The airplane was transferred to the Army's Aberdeen Proving Ground for vulnerability tests in 1956. (USAF)

Korea: Limited War

On Sunday, June 25, 1950, the Communist North Koreans began a major offensive against the Republic of Korea, spearheaded by Russian-built tanks. To the south, on Okinawa, was the once mighty 20th Air Force. Its B-29 force, the 19th Bomb Group, was at Andersen Air Base on Guam; the 19th had just twenty-two bombers.

When General Douglas MacArthur was instructed to support South Korea he wanted the air force into action immediately, and the 19th was ordered to Kadena on Okinawa. Nineteen hours after the receipt of these orders, the 19th struck the opening B-29 blow of the Korean War, when four aircraft were sent to the Munsan area to look for targets of opportunity.

As the B-29s pecked away at tactical targets, the news was getting gloomier. President Truman wanted to insure that the bombing was not "indiscriminate", and plans to wipe out North Korean targets with incendiaries were not approved. A trend emerged in Korea that there was no specific military objective, and that some targets were "sensitive", and some tactics had "far-reaching political implications".

As the situation worsened, two SAC B-29 groups, the 22nd and 92nd, were ordered to the Far East. To control the strategic bombers theEast Air Forces Bomber Command was set up at Yokota, Japan, with General "Rosie" O'Donnell commanding.

The North Korean forces gained most of their support from beyond Korea, where the bombers could not go, so the effects of a strategic air campaign could not be conclusive. However, North Korea had five major industrial centers, one of the world's major hydroelectric complexes and other scattered strategic targets. A short, sharp campaign was begun in July 1950, but it was hampered by tactical demands on the B-29s. At the end of July it was proposed to send two more groups, the 98th and 307th, on condition that they were used specifically for strategic purposes, and by the middle of September the major targets had been neutralized. The B-29s also proved that they could methodically destroy the enemy's transport system, including bridges, and O'Donnell was able to boast that his bombers had knocked out all but seven of forty-four key highway and railway bridges, and the other seven were unusable.

The B-29s flew intensive interdiction missions in support of the amphibious landing at Inchon, and strangled the enemy rail system.

With the situation apparently under control, the 22nd and 92nd Groups were released for return to the States and the other groups were told they would probably depart early in December.

However, there had been a massive buildup of Chinese forces along the Yalu River, and in view of the ominous situation MacArthur ordered two weeks of maximum strikes to destroy the "Korean ends" of all the international bridges over the Yalu to Manchuria. The bridges were a complicated target, and as November progressed it was increasingly evident that the end was not justifying the means. While the bombing was in progress the Chinese threw pontoon bridges across the river, and the Yalu was already beginning to freeze over.

The operations near the border encountered sporadic but effective fighter opposition, then in late November the war took a dramatic turn. A huge Chinese regular force streamed into Korea, and the United Nations units were forced to pull back.

Through the early weeks of 1951 the B-29s flew support and interdiction missions, and although the Communists did not generally unleash their MiGs, the Red jets became more active. Then, late in March, the major air clashes which would decide air superiority over northwestern Korea began shaping up. Attacks against the international bridges had been suspended while the Yalu was frozen, but the winter ice was breaking up and the most important of the bridges, at Sinuiju, was dangerously close to the MiG airfield at Antung in Manchuria. The B-29s would need heavy fighter escort. The first big spring mission against the bridges was flown on March 30, and came off well. Only the 19th Group suffered serious interference, and its gunners claimed two MiGs. In a final effort to get the Sinuiju railway bridge, all three B-29 groups went there on April 12. The bombers were strung out in the target area, causing their F-84 escort to split up and allowing the MiGs to pick out weaker formations. Three minutes from the target the 19th was hit by fifty MiGs. One B-29s crashed in flames and five others were damaged. **Dragon Lady** took a direct hit in the nose which killed the airplane commander and the bombardier and badly wounded the pilot. About twenty MiGs hit the 307th and knocked down one of their B-29s; another struggled back to a crashlanding. The bombers claimed ten MiGs, but three B-29s was too great a cost.

In the first year of war the Communists had taken huge losses, and peace talks began in July 1951. However, these negotiations were fruitless, and there was suspicion that the Communists were getting ready for a major new offensive. In June 1951 the enemy had over 1,000 planes, more than half of them in Manchuria, and towards the end of July it became obvious that they were attempting to gain superiority over "MiG Alley". That area, in northwestern Korea between the Chongchon and Yalu rivers, had been off-limits to unescorted B-29s since the beginning of June.

The peace talks broke down late in August and September began with a major Red air campaign. As the Sabres wrestled the MiGs further north, the B-29s were trying to neutralize the North Korean airfields. They had been flying about sixteen combat sorties a day, mixed missions including airfield and bridge strikes, "Phantom" ground-controlled support missions, radar evaluation, leaflet drops and Shoran missions - a particularly effective technique involving two radio stations in friendly territory transmitting beams which intersected over a chosen enemy target area. The 19th had also tried a new type of ground-controlled radar bombing, "Golfball", very effectively.

It was decided to knock out the airfields quickly with daylight formation attacks, and the missions proved to be perilous. On October 23 the MiGs were ready. South of the Yalu about one hundred took on the screening Sabres, but the Thunderjets with the B-29s refused to be drawn away. The MiGs attacked, and the F-84s could not adequately protect the bombers. Three B-29s went down, and all except one of the others had major damage and dead and wounded aboard.

In October 1951 the old B-29s claimed eight MiGs destroyed. but five bombers had been lost in action, the worst losses of the war. Prior to that bloody month only six had been lost in fifteen months of combat. Even so, the B-29s would bounce back. A solid shield of Sabres simply could not be provided, so a unique solution to the problem was found: the B-29s would operate only at night. By the end of November things were going well, particularly due to the efficiency of Shoran bombing, and only along the Yalu were the Communists able to make things really hot at night. Then in early 1952 the enemy began installing bands of searchlights and flak well south of the older dangers areas along the Yalu. Things warmed up again, and on the moonlit night of June 10, four 19th Group B-29s attacking a railway bridge at Kwaksan were locked and held by over twenty searchlights. One bomber blew up over the target, another went down over North Korea and a third was so badly damaged that it just struggled to a crash landing at Kimpo.

Throughout the summer of 1952, a solution to the problems of flak, fighters and searchlights was sought. The B-29s had been using electronic countermeasures to some degree for over a year, but after the Kwaksan mission, added emphasis was placed on this area. As well, all the B-29s were camouflaged with black gloss lacquer and gun-flash suppressors were acquired and the gunners ordered to return enemy fire.

In the winter months the Communists made no strong challenge for daylight air supremacy, but at night they were much more active against the B-29s. The darkness was no longer giving the bombers enough protection, and by the end of January 1953 the future of the B-29s was again in the balance. Only by taking every possible precaution could they operate with a margin of safety. Attacks were irregularly scheduled, altitudes were varied as much as possible, the bomber stream was compressed, contrail altitudes were avoided, strongly defended targets were hit during the dark of the moon, the planes were camouflaged, friendly night fighters gave support, and electronic countermeasures were extensively used against Red gunlaying and searchlight radar. General William Fisher, then commander of the B-29s, admitted that if the enemy night fighters ever gained an all weather capability "the B-29 business is really going to get rough".

During these tough times the B-29s were involved in probably their oddest job in two wars. On the night of April 26, 1953, a couple dropped more than a million leaflets along the Yalu, offering hefty rewards in Russian, Chinese and Korean to any pilots who would deliver their MiGs to Kimpo airfield. All comers were promised $50,000 and political asylum, with a $50,000 bonus to the first in. "Project Moolah" involved another leaflet drop in May, but the results were negative.

Although the haggling and blood-letting continued, the war was nearing its inconclusive end. As a settlement became imminent the B-29s were involved in an all-out effort to neutralize Red airfields in North Korean, to prevent MiGs moving in immediately prior to the ceasefire.

The armistice was finally signed in the morning of July 27, 1953, to become effective twelve hours later. As a parting shot two 98th Wing Superforts and two 91st Squadron RB-29s flew a "paper route" - dropping psychological warfare leaflets. One of the RB-29 sorties, flown by Lieutenant Denver Cook, was the last B-29 combat mission.

The old B-29s had dropped 185,000 tons of bombs in nearly 22,000 sorties during their second, and last, war.

The 92nd Group's 44-62102, piloted by Captain Leo Moffatt, over the Sea of Japan. (Paul Kelly)

B-29s of the 98th Bomb Group, which fought over Korea from August 1950, head for enemy transportation targets in December 1950. (USAF)

The 22nd Bomb Group's *Never Hoppen*, 44-62196, unloading over North Korea. The 22nd flew its first mission in July 1950, and its last in October of that year. (SAC)

Snugglebunny, 44-69667, was proof that the B-29 was a fine airplane. She had flown her share of missions with the 6th Group from Tinian, then flew seventy-five more with the 98th Group in Korea. (USAF)

On October 23, 1951, the MiGs were ready for the B-29s. Sergeant Frank Bata was right blister gunner on a 307th Group Superfortress that was hit hard by the jet fighters - his blister was shot out, and a large hole was blown in the tail of the airplane. In return his crew got two MiGs, one each credited to the tail and CFC gunners. (Bata)

The massive Tarzon bomb, used by the 19th Group. Each squadron had one specially-modified B-29, and the group dropped thirty of these six-ton bombs before use of Tarzons was suspended in August 1951. (USAF)

Planeloads of high explosive being laid out on the hardstands at Yokota, Japan. In the background is the 98th's Beetle Bomber, **44-69800. August 24, 1951. (USAF)**

The 22nd Group's Spirit of Freeport, **44-62060, returning to Kadena after her twenty-eighth mission. The B-29 was then sent home for a gala reception at Freeport, New York. (USAF)**

So Tired, **44-61727, from the 91st Photo Recon Squadron. Only one RB-29 squadron served in the Korean War, and one of the 91st's aircraft flew the last Superfort mission of the war, dumping psywar leaflets on July 27, 1953. (USAF)**

The 98th over Korea. In the foreground is 45-21721, *Tail Wind*, **from the 344th Squadron. (USAF/Robin Gilbert)**

The 19th's *Command Decision*, **44-87657, was probably the best-known B-29 of the Korean War. She flew 121 missions, and her gunners destroyed five jet fighters, three of them during the savage battle on October 27, 1951. (USAF)**

To counter Communist flak, fighters and searchlights, the aging B-29s tried everything...electronic countermeasures, using bad weather as a cover and, in the summer of 1952, all B-29s were camouflaged with black gloss lacquer. As the B-29s were already operating only at night, the high visibility tail markings were no longer necessary. These are 98th Wing B-29s, moving out at Yokota in March 1953. (USAF)

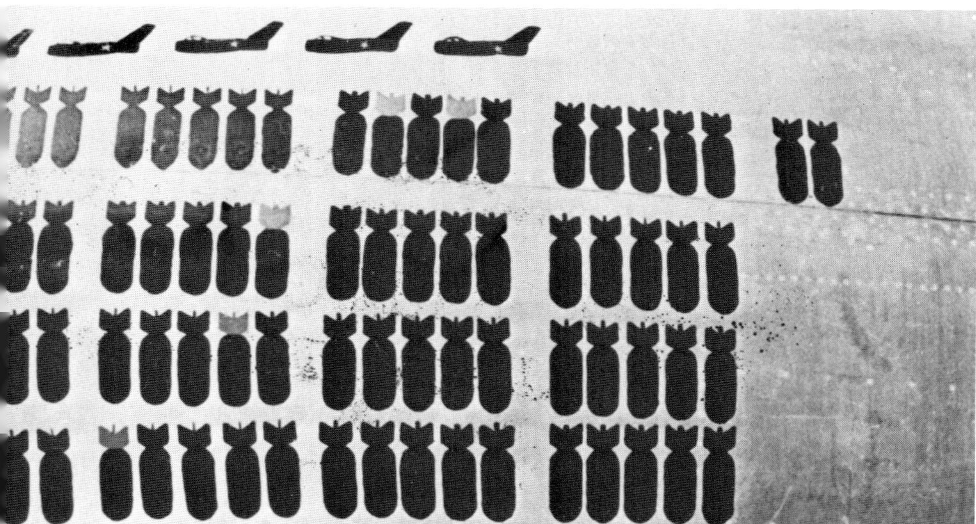

The scoreboard on the 19th Group's 44-61835, Dragon Lady. The bomb stencils with red tails denote lead missions. The five MiG stencils apparently include some which were not officially recognized kills. (Boeing)

Honeybucket Honshos, 44-61929, another 91st Recon RB-29, and carrying caricatures of her entire flight crew. (Earl N. Heath)

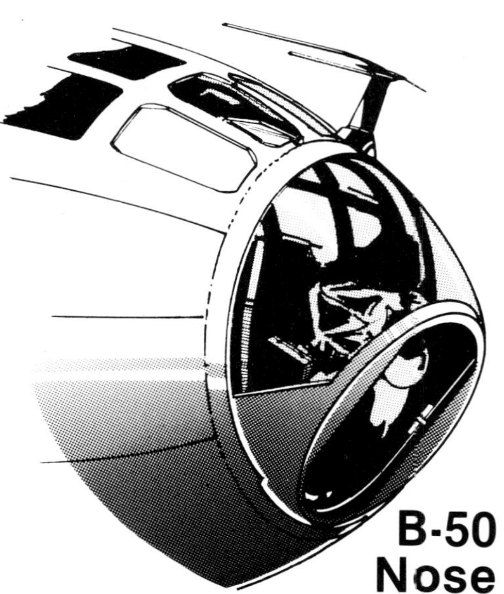

B-50 Nose

Much of the 98th's elaborate nose art was painted by a local Japanese artist, recalled only by the nickname "Rembrandt". It seems ironic that a Japanese would be decorating planes like Nip On Nees, 44-62261, just six or seven years after the B-29s burned Japan to the ground. (Edd Halseth)

44-61533, Salem Witch, an RB-29 from the 91st Strategic Recon Squadron. This squadron was identified by a green tail tip, and green nosewheel doors with a white barb. (Paul Zobrist)

Miss Spokane, 44-27332, flew with the 92nd Group and was passed on to the 98th. (Boeing)

The Duchess Combat Ready, **42-93880, almost survived. After the war and her missions with the 98th, she was ultimately sent to China Lake. In 1975 her nose section, still with the fading name and nose art, went to Tuscon, but it was melted down. (Zobrist)**

(Above left) Space Mistress, **44-86316, from the 344th Squadron of the 98th Wing. (Halseth)**

KB-29s from the 43rd Air Refueling Squadron were sent to Yokota on detached service. Known as "Det 4", the handful of tankers were used to refuel the 91st's RB-45s, and also were involved in combat refueling tests with the F-84s of the 159th Fighter Bomber Squadron during 1952. The tankers were appropriately named - Touch and Go **was serial number 44-87601. (Halseth)**

This B-29, 44-69746, flew its first Korea missions as the 22nd Group's Charlie's Wagon **around October 1950, then went to the 98th, where she became** September Song**. She had also flown with the 500th Bomb Group during the latter days of World War II. (Zobrist)**

Slow Freight 4th, **44-61834 from the 98th, carried the elaborate markings which characterised the unit's B-29s. The ground crew is listed on a plaque as "Knott's Knot Heads", and each aircrew member is identified by position, rank, initials, name and nickname. This aircraft has been fitted with a one-piece B-50 clear nose section. (Halseth)**

Korean War crews were not superstitious about changing a name, or design. Ace In The Hole **and** Sac's Appeal **were two of three designs which appeared on the 98th's 44-61872; the latter is based on an early Marilyn Monroe pinup. (Halseth)**

Hanna-Barbera's Droopy appeared on this stripped down B-29 at Yokota, used for electronic countermeasures work and possibly from the 3rd Radar Calibration Squadron. (Paul D. Stevens)

The black lacquer was carefully applied around the artwork on Shack Rabbit, 44-83934, but the name was changed to Undecided. She flew with the 98th during the Korean War. (Zobrist/Halseth)

Town Pump, 44-27282, was another 43rd Air Refueling Squadron KB-29 tanker assigned to "Det 4" at Yokota during the Korean conflict. (Halseth)

The Other B-29

The B-29 was the subject of one of the most unusual and ambitious projects ever conceived in aviation history: the copying and production of the most sophisticated airplane in the world, by an industry that then could not have begun the design of such an advanced bomber.

In spite of repeated requests by the Soviet Union, Britain and the United States refused to provide examples of modern 4-engined strategic bombers to the Russian Air Force, though many examples of twin-engined medium bombers and attack planes (such as the B-25 and A-20) were supplied under Lend Lease. The Soviet government was very aware that the pre-war designed Pe-8 was dangerously obsolescent. In view of the success of the American and British strategic bombing campaigns, Russia had decided to form a long range strategic bombing force itself, and this made the lack of a suitable modern heavy bomber all the more critical.

In mid-1944, XXBomber Command of the 20th AF began its first bombing offensive against Japan with the B-29, operating from bases in China. As mentioned earlier, part of the reason for these missions was the development of tactics for the Superfortress and the correction of faults and difficulties with these often temperamental aircraft. Adding to the losses from engine fires and other mechanical failures, many Japanese targets in Manchuria and the home islands were defended by flak and fighters. While not as extensive as similar defenses over Europe, these still took a toll of the attacking B-29s.

In late July, 1944, a raid was mounted against the Showa Steel Works at Anshan in Manchuria. Over the target, a B-29-5-BW, **42-6256,** of the 771BS, 462BG, was hit by flak under the right wing, putting number three engine out of commission and starting an oil leak in number four. With only two good engines, the crew followed then - current emergency procedures and headed for Vladivostok in the Soviet Union. Expecting friendly treatment from our ally in Europe - even if Russia was officially neutral in the Pacific - the B-29 crew was surprised to be bounced by Russian fighters, who buzzed the ship and fired tracers across her nose. Under Russian orders, the pilot followed the fighters to a small field and landed his crippled plane. The crew never saw it again.

In November, 1944, two more B-29s, both from the 794BS, 468BG, landed in the Soviet Union, again expecting reasonable treatment from an "allied" nation. All the crews were allowed to "escape" to Iran from a detention camp in Tashkent, but the aircraft, "General H. H. Arnold Special", **42-6365,** and "Ding How", **42-6358,** were interned and never seen again. The Soviet government, though within its legal rights as a neutral to impound aircraft of combatant nations, in fact had impounded these B-29s with the intention of producing an exact copy! At the time, Western observers would have thought Russian aviation companies and engineers completely incapable of producing such a complicated warplane.

In spite of the many great difficulties ahead of them, the Russians tested the three intact aircraft, and then began the involved task of preparing to produce the complete airplane and all its subsidiary systems. The design bureau headed by Audrei Tupelov was given the task of producing the airframes and assembling the finished aircraft. The Shvetsov engine design bureau was ordered to copy the advanced - and still troublesome - Wright R-3350 18-cylinder engine and the General Electric turbosupercharger. Other bureaus received orders to analyze and copy the propellers, wheels and brakes, tires, instruments, radio and radar gear and especially the advanced General Electric computerized fire control system for the five remote controlled power gun turrets. Except for the armament - Russian 12.5mm guns replacing the original .50 Brownings - virtually every piece of the B-29 was copied exactly as it was produced in the United States.

In one of the most ambitious and successful projects in aeronautical production engineering, the B-29s were dismantled into sub-assemblies, then components, and finally individual pieces. The various design bureaus had to solve extremely difficult problems in metal alloy formulation, forging, casting, electronic component production, and conversion of American technology to Russian production practices (and vice versa). In spite of these formidable obstacles, Tupelov and his colleagues succeeded, in less than two years, in producing a number of pre-production aircraft and laying the groundwork for series production.

First reports of this unique achievemont were dismissed by the West as "incredible". The Tushino air show in August 1947 convinced the world that the Russian had done the "impossible". Three "B-29s" were shown, and these could have been explained as being the three captured American ships, except that a transport version - with a new fatter fuselage, but retaining the distinctive B-29 wings, engines and tail surfaces - was also flown, proving that the Russians **had** succeeded in copying the design and producing it.

The Tupelov "B-29" was designated the Tu-4; later, it received the NATO code name "Bull". Several hundred were produced, and for several years it was the Soviets' strategic bomber. Externally the Tu-4 was indistinguishable from the B-29 - so exact was the copy that all panel lines and rivet lines were identical. Various changes were made during the production run as the Russians gained experience with the new technologies the B-29 had given them. Later Tu-4s had twin 23mm cannon in each turret. As all the American B-29s had been early examples, none had the four-gun upper nose turret, so all Tu-4s had the early two-gun turret in this position.

The service life of the Tu-4 roughly paralleled that of the B-29: first used as a strategic bomber, then maritime patrol aircraft, then as a trainer for later types and finally scrapped or expended as targets. However, the Tu-4 was not to fade away completely. The technology found in the B-29s, the new production processes and experience, the engineering experience and knowledge gained in copying this remarkable airplane all contributed to a tremendous leap in Russian aviation technology, and the Tu-4, through a process of long-term development, led directly to the Tu-20 "Bear", Tu-114 airliner, and the Tu-126 "Moss" AWACS patrol plane; a few are still in service

This rare photograph illustrates one of the several hundred production examples of the Tu-4. Externally indistinguishable from the B-29, this example can be identified only by its insignia and the long barrels of the 23mm cannon mounted in the turrets. Note the two gun top forward turret, a legacy of the early production B-29s used as patterns by the Russians. (Zdenek Titz)

Living Memories

Considering that there were fewer than four thousand B-29s built, the Superfortress is quite well represented over thirty years later. There are more than a dozen B-29s flying, about to fly, on display or about to be displayed. Following is a complete list of these, with a brief sketch of their known military careers.

44-62070, now flying with the Confederate Air Force as **Fifi.** Saved from the Naval Weapons Center at China Lake. Originally delivered to USAAF at the end of July 1945, modified to TB-29A in 1946, to desert storage in 1948. Assigned to SAC's 310th Bomb Wing in 1952, to the Navy in 1956. The Confederate Air Force flew her to Harlingen, Texas in 1971.

42-93967, a Renton F-13A which served with the 330th Group on Guam during World War II, presumably as a special weather recon aircraft. Now on display at Georgia Veterans State Park, Cordele, Georgia.

44-84076, a Bell B-29 which flew with the 4754th Radar Evaluation Squadron at Hamilton AFB. Her last flight was July 6, 1959, when she was delivered to the Strategic Aerospace Museum at Offutt AFB, Nebraska, where she is on display.

44-61669, with Yesterday's Air Force at Barstow-Daggett Airport, California. Aircraft previously at China Lake Naval Weapons Center.

44-27297, Bockscar, the Omaha B-29 flew with the 509th Composite Group and dropped the atom bomb on Nagasaki. On display at the Air Force Museum, Wright-Patterson AFB, Ohio.

44-86292, Enola Gray, Colonel Paul Tibbets' 509th Composite Group B-29. Preserved by the National Air and Space Museum in Washington, in their storage facility.

44-61671, originally the first Superfortress to be modified to the SB-29 Air-Sea Rescue configuration. Saved from Aberdeen Proving Ground by SAC's 509th Bomb Wing, as a memorial to the World War II 509th. Restored and displayed at Pease Air Force Base with markings carried by the 509th's **The Great Artiste.**

44-61975, acquired from Aberdeen Proving Ground in 1973 by the Bradley Air Museum in Connecticut. Currently being fully restored.

44-62022, a China Lake aircraft reportedly now at Pueblo Municipal Airport Museum in Colorado.

44-62139, fuselage section used a walk-through exhibit at the Air Force Museum in Ohio. Simulated markings of **Command Decision,** 19th Group, Korean War.

45-21739, a China Lake B-29 donated to the UN Korean War Allies Association and displayed since 1972 at their museum in Seoul, Korea.

A B-29 on display at Chanute Air Force Base in Illinois, currently painted to resemble **Enola Gay;** serial quoted as 45-21749, a 19th Group Tarzon aircraft which was lost March 19, 1951, and previously painted with the tail serial "653347", never a B-29 serial number. Possibly 42-65347, an old 6th Bomb Group aircraft.

45-21787, one of four B-29s which went to the Navy in 1947. Named **Fertile Myrtle** and used for experiments with the Douglas Skyrocket, then used by NACA as mother ship for Bell rocket research aircraft. Fully restored and flyable, she is privately owned by the American Air Museum in Oakland, California.

44-70113, flew with the 500th Group as Z-58, completing 26 missions. Stored at Warner-Robins AFB in Georgia from 1946 until 1951, when she was assigned to the 580th Air Resupply and Communications Squadron. The aircraft moved on to the 582nd Squadron, and operated from Molesworth in England until 1958, when she was flown to Aberdeen Proving Ground. Currently awaiting restoration by the Florence Air & Missile Museum in South Carolina.

44-70016, a veteran of the 330th Bomb Group where she was named **Sentimental Journey** and also carried the 314th Wing name **Quaker-City.** She flew over thirty missions, returned to the US and was put in storage. In March 1951 she was redesignated TB-29 and was assigned to the 1st Radar Calibration Squadron, then in 1954 went to 4713th Revron. In 1959 she was sent to storage at Davis-Monthan, and ten years later loaned to the Pima Air Museum in Arizona, where she is displayed.

44-61748, a Renton B-29, has been saved from China Lake and given to the Imperial War Museum in England. This aircraft flew with the 307th Bomb Group in Korea and still carries faded traced of their markings, although since her combat days she had served as a trainer and target tug.

The Pima Air Museum's B-29, with temporary insignia. She was taken overseas by Lieutenant Lester Gilbert and his crew and was the 330th Group's "K-40" on Guam. (Rhodes Arnold)

Fertile Myrtle, **one of the two B-29s still flying, in 1972. (Joe Kucera)**

The Confederate Air Force's Fifi **at the 58th Wing reunion at Minneapolis in 1978. She appears regularly at air shows and portrayed** Enola Gay **in a British television documentary. (Charles B. Mayer)**